WAR
AND
PEACE

A Summary of
Leo Tolstoy's Classic Novel

Nicole Rivett Howeson

War and Peace 100 page summaries
copyright © by 100 page summaries.

All rights reserved.
Printed in the United States of America.

ISBN: 978-1-939370-05-1

Library of Congress Cataloging-in-Publication Data

Howeson, Nicole Rivett
War and Peace A Summary of Leo Tolstoy's Classic Novel/Nicole Rivett Howeson

This publication is designed to provide accurate and authoritative information in regard to the subject matter covered. It is sold with the understanding that neither the author nor the publisher is registered experts in the subject matter discussed. If legal advice or other expert assistance is required, the services of a competent professional person should be sought.

Table of Contents

Short Summary

Love, faith, history, power, money, politics, lust, nature, friendship, trust, patriotism, doubt, happiness, betrayal, strategy, and destiny: a book that explores all of these themes and more must be very long indeed. In fact, it takes approximately 560,000 words to tell the story. The book is *War and Peace*.

Perhaps more famous for its length than its content, *War and Peace* is a daring, ambitious epic set against the background of the Napoleonic wars in Europe during 1805-1812. The author, Leo Tolstoy, himself said about it that, "It is not a novel, even less is it a poem, and still less an historical chronicle." Yet the book contains all of those things, along with philosophical and religious meditations, sketches of nature and simple village life, outlines of military strategy, satire of the aristocracy, and much more. In fact, with this book, Tolstoy invented a new literary genre, historical fiction, in which fictional characters live through real historical events and interact with actual historical figures. Tolstoy weaves together nearly 600 characters' stories, among them Napoleon and Emperor Alexander I, into one tapestry of human experience. American novelist Henry James declared, "Tolstoy is a reflector as vast as a natural lake; a monster harnessed to his great subject—all human life!"

War and Peace is famous for its length, its complexity, and its many characters. At its core, though, it is the journey of one impetuous young man set against the backdrop of a tumultuous, war-torn period in history. Perhaps unsurprisingly, that young man, Pierre Bezukhov, bears no small resemblance to the author himself (as do several of the other characters). Furthermore, Tolstoy was particularly qualified to write the stories of the wars of 1805-1812 from the perspective of the combatants, having fought in the Crimean War himself. In fact, when he wrote journalistic accounts of the battles for newspapers back home, he launched his literary career and found the style and subjects about which he would write for the rest of his life.

The book begins in 1805 in St. Petersburg, Russia. Pierre Bezukhov returns from Europe just as news is breaking of Napoleon's conquests there. His friend, Andrew Bolkonski, heads to the front to escape the ennui of his life. Pierre's acquaintances in Moscow, the Rostov family, also send their son, Nicholas, to the war front. The war will change the lives of these young men (and their extended families) immeasurably. As the years pass, the characters cannot help but be affected by and entangled in the political and social events taking place in their country. Finally, each of them ends up in the decisive Battle of Borodino.

The novel works on two levels: the zoomed-in personal stories and the wide-angle view of the nations and leaders of Europe, with their hundreds of thousands of soldiers fighting one another. There are parallel plots, with their respective conflicts. On the national level, Napoleon's armies triumphantly take control of much territory in Europe, including Russia's allies in Austria and Prussia; in response, Russia declares war against France and they fight a series of battles. The two Emperors, Alexander I of Russia and Napoleon I of France, experience similar problems, with shortages and lack of order among their troops, so a truce seems inevitable. Indeed, a peace agreement is signed, but then Napoleon invades Prussia, pulling Russia back into war. Napoleon and his troops advance on Moscow. Finally, at the Battle of Borodino, the tide shifts and Russia begins driving back the French.

At the same time, on the level of individual characters, Pierre, Andrew, Nicholas, Andrew's sister, Mary, and Nicholas' sister, Natasha, all struggle through life while trying to maintain their ideals, happiness, and moral integrity in the face of grief, injustice, and disillusionment. Additionally, the great leaders of the world are shown to be just as human and fallible as the protagonists of the story. Tolstoy depicts the triumphs, shortcomings, and eccentricities of Alexander, Napoleon, and General Kutuzov. He takes issue with the way the history of the war had been told in the past; he incorporates a new perspective on real events into his fictional narrative. The outcome of the wars is, in his opinion, inevitable. It was not the will of one or two "great" people. Scores of people, thousands of small decisions created the outcome; however, the journey to reach that outcome is fascinating and emotionally powerful, both for the individual characters and for the large armies at war.

BOOK ONE

1805

Book 1: Chapters 1-5

What Happens?

The novel begins in the middle of a conversation. Anna Pavlovna Scherer, a well-connected socialite, is hosting a party at her home in St. Petersburg in July 1805. She speaks to one of her guests, Prince Vasili Kuragin, about Napoleon, whom she regards as the Antichrist, and declares that Russia alone must save Europe. The conversation turns to other matters, including Vasili's children: his beautiful daughter, Helene, and his two dissolute sons, Hippolyte and Anatole. Anna suggests marrying off Anatole to a rich, unhappy relative, Princess Mary Bolkonskaya. Mary's sister-in-law, Lise, is at the party, and captivates everyone there. There is a newcomer to the social circle present as well—Pierre Bezukhov, the illegitimate but favorite son of the elderly Count Bezukhov, who was raised abroad and has recently returned to Russia. He and Prince Andrew Bolkonski, Lise's husband, are close friends. His presence is the only aspect of the party which cheers Andrew up; they are also the only two admirers of Napoleon present. Andrew, though, will soon leave the city to serve as adjutant or aide-de-camp to General Kutuzov. Also in attendance is Princess Anna Mikhaylovna Drubetskaya, an impoverished widow who begs Vasili to obtain a less dangerous commission in the military for her only son, Boris. She reminds him that he owes the start of his career to her family. The party concludes after Pierre makes an inappropriately long and opinionated defense of Napoleon, and Hippolyte Kuragin defuses the social tension by telling a pointless story.

Analysis:

Tolstoy introduces us to the characters at the party the way we would meet them if we were attending the party ourselves. We learn their names, but must observe their behavior and listen to their conversations to really learn anything about them. Some characters are insincere or phony; for instance, Princess Helene Kuragina's smile never changes, even as she talks to different people. Others are so shaped by society that they have few opinions of their own. A few, though, are honest and genuine, and it is clear that the author prefers them. Pierre is one such character, and he is socially awkward (though still liked by others) as a result. Andrew is quieter about his opinions, and therefore makes fewer waves in society, but all the same, he cannot conceal his feelings. He is bored at the party and even repulsed by his wife—whom nearly everyone else adores—but genuinely happy to see Pierre there.

Key Takeaways:

"'Well, Prince, so Genoa and Lucca are now just family estates of the Buonapartes. But I warn you, if you don't tell me that this means war, if you still try to defend the infamies and horrors perpetrated by that Antichrist—I really believe he is Antichrist—I will have nothing more to do with you and you are no longer my friend, no longer my 'faithful slave,' as you call yourself! But how do you do? I see I have frightened you—sit down and tell me all the news.'" The novel begins with Anna Pavlovna Scherer making this abrupt declaration. Her word choices and manner of speaking reveal much about her and the society she represents: by calling Napoleon by the Italian version of his surname, instead of the French, she underscores the perception that he is an upstart, an imposter to the French throne. Her belief in his being the Antichrist hints that she has but shallow understanding of politics (and religion)—but this idea will prove to be an important one later in the novel.

"'I was told a charming Moscow story today and must treat you to it. Excuse me, Vicomte—I must tell it in Russian or the point will be lost...' And Prince Hippolyte began to tell his story in such Russian as a Frenchman would speak after spending about a year in Russia." This is the first of many such situations to which Tolstoy will carefully call the reader's attention: Hippolyte, and many other members of the Russian elite, speak Russian poorly. For decades, Russian society has adopted French culture, and has looked down upon the native Russian culture and language. The novel features several key scenes in which characters find their way back to their "Russianness."

Book 1: Chapters 6-9

What Happens?

As they take their leave of Anna Pavlovna, Hippolyte flirts shamelessly with Lise, despite the situation being made doubly awkward by her advanced state of pregnancy and her husband being present. Pierre follows Andrew and Lise to their house, where the two men can have a more personal conversation. The most urgent matter to discuss is that Pierre's father expects him to choose a career soon, but he cannot decide on anything. Andrew suggests joining the military, as he himself has done. He admits that he is unhappy with the pretty, vapid wife he married, and is going to war to escape her and the rest of society like her.

Lise interrupts their conversation. In an extraordinary scene, Pierre unknowingly brings up the one topic that is tormenting her, and she must discuss it with Andrew even though there is a guest present. She is not her husband's equal intellectually, but she understands that he is running away from her to go to the war. She does not know what she has done to deserve this rejection, but she is terrified to leave her friends and give birth at the home of Andrew's father and sister—without Andrew there. Andrew insists that she go to bed.

Rather unreasonably, he makes Pierre promise not to get married, and not to join his dissipated friends in their revelry. Pierre immediately breaks the latter promise when he leaves the Bolkonskis' home. He goes to a wild party at Anatole Kuragin's home, where the revelers are teasing a bear cub and one officer, Dolokhov, drinks a bottle of rum while precariously balanced on a window ledge.

Analysis:

Thoughts of war are ever-present in the characters' lives, but even more striking are the similarities of their peacetime society to a battlefield—similarities they themselves may not perceive. There is a constant struggle for social power, and battles do occasionally take place, although they are fought with whispers of gossip and bestowing of favors, rather than literal weapons. Pierre's situation in society is an unhappy one indeed because, as an illegitimate son, he lacks material resources and social standing, and, unlike many other members of society, he is not a conniving strategist who can better his situation through alliances with better-connected people. Andrew was born with all of the things Pierre lacks—property, noble birth, intelligence, perseverance—but finds social climbing distasteful. In turn, Andrew envies Pierre's freedom from family obligations and personal history. The bizarre promises he asks from Pierre—that he will not marry until he is too old to care about anything, and that he will give up his troublemaker friends—make sense in the light of his own wish to be free of his wife and social circle.

Key Takeaways:

"'There is a war now against Napoleon. If it were a war for freedom I could understand it and should be the first to enter the army; but to help England and Austria against the greatest man in the world is not right.'

'If no one fought except on his own conviction, there would be no wars,' he [Andrew] said.

'And that would be splendid,' said Pierre."

At the party, Pierre's intelligent—though socially indelicate—questions and opinions may have distracted the reader from the fact that he is only twenty years old, but in these chapters he reveals his immaturity and naiveté. He and Andrew both believe in the theory that "great men" direct history, and that Napoleon is one such man. *War and Peace* will chronicle their divergent journeys over the coming years, and both of their views will evolve regarding Napoleon.

"'I have long wanted to ask you, Andrew, why you have changed so to me? What have I done to you? You are going to the war and have no pity for me. Why is it?'" These words with which Lise confronts Andrew will be echoed later, in a more important context.

Book 1: Chapters 10-21

What Happens?

Anna Mikhaylovna Drubetskaya goes to the home of her relatives, Count Ilya Rostov and his family, in Moscow. Prince Vasili Kuragin had successfully procured her son, Boris, the transfer she requested at Anna Pavlovna Scherer's party. The Rostovs are hosting a name-day party—a celebration held on the feast day of the saint after whom a person was named (in the 19th century in Russia, name-day celebrations were more popular than birthday celebrations). The guests gossip about Pierre, who, it seems, got into trouble with the police that night he went drinking with Dolokhov and Kuragin. His father is now on his deathbed.

The younger generation enters the drawing room—the count's four children, Vera, Nicholas, Natasha, and Petya, along with their cousin, Sonya Rostova, and Boris Drubetskoy. The young people are much livelier than the dull guests, who talk only of problems and seem to bore even their hosts, the count and countess. Privately, Boris promises Natasha that in four years, he will ask for her hand. Meanwhile, his mother decides to leave the party to see if the dying Count Bezukhov will leave an inheritance to Boris, his godson. While his mother tries to force her way into the invalid's room, Boris speaks with Pierre, who is being shunned by the rest of the relatives at the house. He invites him to dinner at the Rostovs.'

Countess Rostova, meanwhile, decides to give Anna Mikhaylovna the money she needs to equip Boris for his new commission, though the Rostovs, it is hinted, can hardly spare the money (or afford this lavish party). The Moscow counterpart to Anna Scherer, Countess Marya Dmitrievna Akhrosimova, arrives, and dinner finally begins, followed by singing, card games and dancing. Dinner conversation mainly focuses on the war. In a jolly final scene of the party, the portly pair of Count Rostov and Marya Dmitrievna dance an English dance that had been popular when they were young.

Analysis:

The reader is taken to another party, quite different from the first. The Rostovs are generous, kind-hearted people, and they do not control their guests' or their children's behavior in the dictatorial manner in which Anna Pavlovna Scherer does. The children and adolescents in the home experience all manner of emotions, from infatuation to irritation to jealousy to enthusiasm for the pleasures of food and dancing. When the war is discussed, it is young Nicholas who speaks with patriotism: "I am convinced that we Russians must die or conquer," he declares at dinner. Tolstoy alternates from scenes of these young people and their concerns to scenes at the home of the dying Count Bezukhov, who is surrounded by people who claim not to want anything from him, yet clearly hope to lay their hands on his fortune. Death, it seems the author wants to remind us, is just as much a part of life as eating, drinking, dancing, laughing, and falling in love. The ones to be pitied are not the children with their heartaches and petty squabbles, or the dying old man, but rather those in between, such as Prince Vasili, Anna Mikhaylovna, and the count's three nieces, who have devoted all their time and energy to selfish concerns and have ceased to experience life fully.

Key Takeaways:

"*How plainly all these young people wear their hearts on their sleeves!*" Anna Mikhaylovna and some of the other guests obviously disapprove of the attachments formed between Nicholas and Sonya, and between Boris and Natasha. Yet the contrasting world of adult behavior, driven by ulterior motives and not emotions, hardly seems preferable to the earnest feelings of the younger generation. Love will be a key theme in this novel, a driving force for much of what happens.

"*But I just wish to say, to avoid misunderstandings, that you are quite mistaken if you reckon me or my mother among such people. We are very poor, but for my own part at any rate, for the very reason that your father is rich, I don't regard myself as a relation of his, and neither I nor my mother would ever ask or take anything from him.*" No doubt through the necessity caused by his poverty, Boris has learned how to behave in society and how to set others at ease. Through this speech, he impresses Pierre with his courage for speaking plainly, and he manages to transfer the awkwardness of his position to Pierre, even though none of what he says is actually true. By befriending Pierre, Boris shows more foresight than other relatives, who treat him badly, only to regret their rudeness when Pierre inherits the lion's share of his father's estate.

Book 1: Chapters 22-24

What Happens?

While the name-day party continues with card games and dancing, Count Bezukhov suffers another stroke. Prince Vasili and one of the Mamontova sisters (the count's nieces) discuss the possibility that Pierre may have been made the legitimate heir. Pierre returns to the house, accompanied by Anna Mikhaylovna, who ensures that he is admitted to see his father. Last rites are performed. Pierre has a final moment of connection with his father, who seems to smile at the horror Pierre feels in seeing how helpless the once-vital man is. Pierre begins to cry quietly.

Meanwhile, Prince Vasili and Princess Catherine Mamontova seek to destroy the will that leaves everything to Pierre, and the accompanying letter that petitions the Emperor to make him a legitimate son. The rather comical scene with Anna Mikhaylovna and Princess Catherine struggling over the portfolio that contains the documents is ended with the news that the count has died.

It seems Pierre will indeed be a rich man soon. Anna Mikhaylovna loses no time in reminding Pierre that she prevented the schemers from taking his inheritance away, and that the old man's wishes were to take care of her Boris.

Analysis:

This is the first scene of death in the novel, but it will be far from the last. Because of the count's wealth and power, he has many people taking care of him, and even more people are merely present in his home, waiting. Soon, though, many lives will be lost at the warfront, with no such ceremony. Although one injustice is averted—Pierre receives the inheritance his father intended for him—there are still many ways in which this situation is unfair. Pierre is not the only illegitimate child of his father, yet it is only he whom his father sought to legitimize. Prince Vasili may possibly have saved Boris's life by procuring him a less dangerous commission, but Anna Mikhaylovna seems to forget the debt she owes him and instead gossips about his bad behavior to Pierre. Now that he is to be a wealthy man, it seems everyone has forgotten Pierre's recent incident with the police in Petersburg, but he does not hold their former hostility to him against them.

Key Takeaways:

"When Pierre came up the count was gazing straight at him, but with a look the significance of which could not be understood by mortal man. Either this look meant nothing but that as long as one has eyes they must look somewhere, or it meant too much. Pierre hesitated, not knowing what to do, and glanced inquiringly at his guide. Anna Mikhaylovna made a hurried sign with her eyes, glancing at the sick man's hand and moving her lips as if to send it a kiss. Pierre, carefully stretching his neck so as not to touch the quilt, followed her suggestion and pressed his lips to the large boned, fleshy hand." The non-Russianness of Russian society is a theme that shows up repeatedly in War and Peace. Pierre is constantly at a loss at key moments, and in many forms of social interaction. Pierre was raised abroad and does not know the traditions of Russian Orthodox worship, or social customs specific to Russian society. Worse still, he does not know how to protect himself from the pitfalls and predators in this society still so new to him.

"'Ah, my friend!' said he, taking Pierre by the elbow; and there was in his voice a sincerity and weakness Pierre had never observed in it before. 'How often we sin, how much we deceive, and all for what? I am near sixty, dear friend... I too... All will end in death, all! Death is awful...' and he burst into tears." Prince Vasili has been a shallow person all his life, and apparently watching the death of a close associate has forced him to become aware of his own mortality for the first time. The fact that he can say this without apology to the young man he was trying to cheat out of his inheritance shows, however, that he is still blissfully free of the naggings of a conscience. If anything, he will return to his social maneuvering with a renewed energy, knowing his time for securing his children's fortunes is finite.

Book 1: Chapters 25-28

What Happens?

The scene next moves to Bald Hills, an estate about 100 miles from Moscow, owned by Prince Nicholas Andreevich Bolkonski, Andrew's father. He is a strict taskmaster, and his small household—his daughter, Mary, her companion, Mademoiselle Bourienne, and the servants—follows an unchanging schedule of activity. Mary receives a letter from Julie Karagina, who had been at the Rostovs' name-day party and has all the news about Pierre. She also warns Mary about the plan for Anatole Kuragin to marry her for her money. Mary replies that she feels sorry for Pierre because of all the temptations money will bring, and that if it is God's will for her to marry, she will try to perform her duties to the best of her ability. Andrew and Lise arrive, and the two sisters-in-law are overjoyed at seeing one another again, though they had only met once before.

The old prince invites his architect to dinner with the family, as some sort of object lesson in equality. He holds court with his opinions on Napoleon, that he is not a "great man" but merely has had poor opponents, with which no one argues because all know it would be pointless. Lise is nearly as terrified of him as she is of childbirth. After dinner, Andrew prepares to leave the next day to go to war. His sister persuades him to take an icon, though it means little to him. Mary tries to convince him to be kinder to Lise. As he departs, his father tries not to show his sadness, shouting at him instead. Lise faints and the little family is left in disarray as Book One concludes.

Analysis:

After two parties and a deathbed vigil, Tolstoy now takes us to the place where there are almost never special events, only unending order and routine. Unlike the party scenes, Tolstoy gives us an extended character description of Prince Nicholas Bolkonski. He is the polar opposite of so many of the other members of high society—while they are chiefly engaged in social events and spending money, the elderly man works long hours "improving" himself, his family, and his estate. Others, like Count Rostov, delegate estate management to employees, and employ governesses and tutors, but Bolkonski will not hear of such things. His avant-garde ideas, and the bluntness with which he espouses them, sheds some light on why Andrew does not conceal his contempt for those intellectually inferior to him. Prince Bolkonski embodies many features of "enlightenment" thinking—love of mathematics and engineering, disregard for sentimentality, mysticism, and religion—but they have only served to make his family lonely and unhappy, Mary particularly so. Andrew is obviously fond of his eccentric father, but at the same time, he cannot stop criticizing him to Mary. He still struggles to establish his own personality, out of his father's shadow. Mary herself is an interesting character—while she does not have the vivaciousness of Natasha Rostov, or the forthrightness of Pierre Bezukhov, she has a stronger moral compass than most of the other characters. With all of the discussions of war so far in the book, she is the only one to have pointed out that the cost in human lives is too high.

Key Takeaways:

"He was himself always occupied: writing his memoirs, solving problems in higher mathematics, turning snuffboxes on a lathe, working in the garden, or superintending the building that was always going on at his estate." Prince Bolkonski's occupations are similar to Tolstoy's own on his estate, Yasnaya Polyana (Sunlit Meadows).

"The old prince seemed convinced not only that all the men of the day were mere babies who did not know the A B C of war or of politics, and that Bonaparte was an insignificant little Frenchy, successful only because there were no longer any Potemkins or Suvorovs left to oppose him; but he was also convinced that there were no political difficulties in Europe and no real war, but only a sort of puppet show at which the men of the day were playing, pretending to do something real." When the talk inevitably turns to war, the old prince shows contempt for Napoleon, but also for the modern era. It seems he believes in the idea of "great men" who are powerful enough to change history—he just does not believe that Napoleon is one of them.

"'No, it can't be helped, lad,' said the prince. 'They're all like that; one can't unmarry. Don't be afraid; I won't tell anyone, but you know it yourself.'" Prince Bolkonski has recognized Andrew's feelings toward his wife, and this both pleases and displeases Andrew. The father means well, as did Mary when she intervened. They are a loving family, although a bit unorthodox.

BOOK TWO

1805

Book 2: Chapters 1-3

What Happens?

Book Two begins in Braunau, Austria, where the Russian troops have arrived after marching hundreds of miles. They are diligently preparing for inspection by General Kutuzov, accompanied by his adjutant, Prince Andrew Bolkonski, but they cannot do much about their boots being in tatters. Kutuzov, though, does not want his men to look too ready to fight, trying to keep the Austrians engaged with the French as long as possible. They change back into their marching uniforms.

The inspection calls attention to one character already known to readers. Dolokhov, Pierre's drinking companion who had perched on the ledge while consuming a bottle of rum, has been demoted to the rank of private, and has been censured for wearing the wrong color uniform. Kutuzov locates him and encourages him to earn his former rank back.

Kutuzov's plan to delay is foiled when the Austrians are defeated at Ulm. The Russian troops will have to go to combat sooner than anyone anticipated. When the news arrives, Andrew immediately understands that half the campaign has been lost and he is deeply grieved. Another officer, Zherkov, makes a joke in front of the defeated Austrian General Mack, and Andrew threatens him.

Analysis:

Although historical fiction is commonplace now, in the 19th century, Tolstoy's device of combining fictional characters and scenes with actual historical figures and events was groundbreaking. Nineteenth-century readers of the novel would have been surprised to find well-known historical figures like Kutuzov interacting with the characters created by Tolstoy's imagination. The author chooses to portray him as being most concerned with the welfare of his troops, and his brilliant military strategies follow from that primary focus.

Key Takeaways:

"'One thing I ask of your excellency,' Dolokhov said in his firm, ringing, deliberate voice. 'I ask an opportunity to atone for my fault and prove my devotion to His Majesty the Emperor and to Russia!'" Dolokhov's sincerity is always questionable, and this speech is no exception. It does not seem to impress Kutuzov, but the fact that the general took an interest in Dolokhov's case makes some of the other officers who had been treating him coolly suddenly behave in a much friendlier manner to him.

"Prince Andrew bowed his head in token of having understood from the first not only what had been said but also what Kutuzov would have liked to tell him." Although Andrew makes little effort to be liked by other officers, he and Kutuzov develop a close and friendly working relationship. Andrew feels energized by having real work to do.

Book 2: Chapters 4-8

What Happens?

Two miles outside of Braunau, Nicholas Rostov is stationed with the Pavlograd regiment of hussars, or light cavalry soldiers. He shares quarters with his commanding officer, Denisov, and the two are on friendly terms. Money is stolen from underneath Denisov's pillow, with only three possible suspects. Nicholas knows the thief must be Telyanin, and confronts him in public, but is disgusted when he starts to cry and lets him keep the money.

Nicholas then reports him to the regimental commander—but again makes the mistake of doing so in front of other officers. Others tell Nicholas to apologize for this breach of etiquette, but he refuses. He does not understand how accusing one person throws the whole regiment into a bad light. The incident grows more awkward, and Nicholas's honor is saved only by the order that the Russian army will march to join the Austrian troops. They move back toward Vienna, and the enemy army comes into view. They fire a measuring shot that falls so short that the Russians know it is safe to keep crossing the bridge they are on. The troops are so disorderly that some wagons and horsemen block others' passage on the bridge, creating a bottleneck.

Finally only Denisov's squadron remains to cross the bridge, but the enemy has drawn closer. They manage to cross and then burn the bridge while under fire, but three men are hit in the process. Nicholas realizes how much danger he is in, and is paralyzed with fear. When the attack is over and the bridge burned, the men move on, and no one seems to care about Nicholas's panic.

Analysis:

Just as the drawing rooms of Petersburg and Moscow are, in their own way, battlefields, so, too, the army barracks have their own social customs and intricacies. Both Nicholas and Andrew went to war expecting simple, single-minded activities, but these idealized notions do not materialize for either of them. The social order of the military is even more complex than the circles they moved in at home: for the first time, they cannot depend on class distinctions to guide their behavior. Nicholas in particular needs to humble himself before men of lower-class backgrounds but higher military rankings than himself.

Key Takeaways:

"I'm not to blame that the conversation began in the presence of other officers. Perhaps I ought not to have spoken before them, but I am not a diplomatist. That's why I joined the hussars, thinking that here one would not need finesse; and he tells me that I am lying—so let him give me satisfaction..." Here we see just how indulgent an upbringing Nicholas had—he sees only his point of view in the matter, and to him it does not seem ludicrous, as it does to the other officers, that he should challenge someone who far outranks him. His family enjoyed great privilege, but that will not always be the case.

"One step beyond that boundary line which resembles the line dividing the living from the dead lies uncertainty, suffering, and death. And what is there? Who is there?—there beyond that field, that tree, that roof lit up by the sun? No one knows, but one wants to know. You fear and yet long to cross that line, and know that sooner or later it must be crossed and you will have to find out what is there, just as you will inevitably have to learn what lies the other side of death. But you are strong, healthy, cheerful, and excited, and are surrounded by other such excitedly animated and healthy men.' So thinks, or at any rate feels, anyone who comes in sight of the enemy, and that feeling gives a particular glamour and glad keenness of impression to everything that takes place at such moments." Tolstoy evidently draws on his own experiences in the Crimean War here, but he does not place the thoughts directly in the mouth of Nicholas Rostov. Instead, he elevates them to the level of the universal, as he will continue to do with scenes of war.

Book 2: Chapters 9-12

What Happens?

The French army is following the Russian troops, trying to engage them in battle. Kutuzov only permits the rear guard to fight, saving the majority of the troops for larger battles later. Finally, they are able to cross the Danube. They then defeat Mortier's division of the French army, the only division on the same side of the river as they are. The battle boosts morale, though a third of the troops were disabled and now all are in a worse state than before.

Prince Andrew, like Nicholas, has his first taste of gunpowder. The Austrian general whom Andrew was assisting is killed, and Andrew's own horse is shot out from under him. A bullet also grazes his arm. Still elated from his combat experience, Andrew is sent to Brunn to tell the Austrian commander of the Russians' victory, but they are not impressed. He lodges with an acquaintance, the diplomat, Bilibin, who explains more about the politicking behind the uneasy alliances between the nations of Europe. Now that Vienna is occupied, Bilibin expects Austria to make peace with the French and turn against Russia.

After running into Hippolyte Kuragin, the man who openly flirted with Lise, Andrew is presented to the Emperor Francis. He is enjoying the hospitality of the dignitaries in Brunn, but he learns that, thanks to another tricky maneuver by Napoleon, not only are the French marching on Brunn, but, worse still, Kutuzov's troops are in a dangerous position, so he returns to them as quickly as he can.

Analysis:

These chapters mark a turning point for Andrew, one that will steer the course of the next years of his life. He has done what he set out to do—to find some kind of purpose, some activity that would allow him to use his talents and abilities. Yet, he immediately learns how hollow these pursuits can be, how little they mean to others who can only see from perspectives of self-interest.

Key Takeaways:

"*He closed his eyes, and immediately a sound of cannonading, of musketry and the rattling of carriage wheels seemed to fill his ears, and now again drawn out in a thin line the musketeers were descending the hill, the French were firing, and he felt his heart palpitating as he rode forward beside Schmidt with the bullets merrily whistling all around, and he experienced tenfold the joy of living, as he had not done since childhood.*

"*He woke up...*

"*'Yes, that all happened!' he said, and, smiling happily to himself like a child, he fell into a deep, youthful slumber.*" Despite the uneasiness about how the war will turn out, and disillusionment about the leaders' failure to honor accomplishments, Andrew finds happiness in the immediate experiences of combat. He is finally, after a lifetime of military-style training from his father, learning what all the routines are for: the completely unpredictable battlefield, which through its danger is life-affirming.

"*'I am speaking sincerely as a friend! Consider! Where and why are you going, when you might remain here? You are faced by one of two things,'*" and the skin over his left temple puckered, '*either you will not reach your regiment before peace is concluded, or you will share defeat and disgrace with Kutuzov's whole army.'*" Despite all of Andrew's pretentions to being cold and rational, he cannot look at the situation as realistically as Bilibin does here. Andrew still has notions of being a war hero, leading the army out of a crisis. No doubt he seeks more feelings of happiness, as he felt at the last battle. Bilibin, in contrast, packs his bags and heads for safety.

Book 2: Chapters 13-21

What Happens?

Andrew meets the army at Krems, where they are in chaos. They are tired and poorly equipped, so Kutuzov sends Prince Bagration's vanguard of four thousand men to stall the French and sends the rest on a 24-hour march to meet other troops at Znaim. Andrew wants to join Bagration's men, but Kutuzov insists that he stay with the retreating army. The plan turns out not to be hopeless after all: French General Murat sees Bagration's vanguard and assumes that many more of Kutuzov's troops are descending upon him, and so he sues for peace. Napoleon, seeing Murat's mistake, sends an angry letter, calling for him to break the armistice and attack. Andrew, meanwhile, finally gets permission to join Bagration's men. At the camp, he meets the humble, odd Captain Tushin, who is getting reprimanded for walking around without boots. He sees a soldier getting flogged for stealing, and observes the French and Russian soldiers talking and arguing with one another across the fence—and one of the Russians is Dolokhov.

Later that night, Andrew's reflections are interrupted by cannon volleys. The French have launched a surprise attack and appear poised to overrun the Russians with sheer numbers, but they are so disorganized that the Russians manage to hold them off for some time. Bagration leads his troops into battle the next morning and Andrew observes how his passive, reactive leadership style gives his men confidence in themselves. Nicholas Rostov's regiment is again unlucky—Zherkov fails to deliver orders to them to retreat. Captain Tushin and his gunners are abandoned but hold their position until Andrew reaches them. Nicholas is wounded.

As the dead and wounded are collected, including Nicholas, Bagration demands to know why Tushin lost his guns. Andrew intervenes to help him avoid punishment, but he is disgusted that no one sees how heroic Tushin was—not even Tushin himself. Meanwhile, Dolokhov repeatedly calls attention to his act of taking a French soldier prisoner in hopes of getting himself promoted. The French do not renew their attack the next day.

Analysis:

These chapters bring everyone's lofty ideals down to earth—even Napoleon's. Tolstoy includes the actual letter Napoleon wrote to Murat, condemning his actions in calling an armistice with the Russians. His frustration that none of the parties involved knew that they did not have the authority to call such a truce suggests the unpreparedness of the leadership on both sides. The battle then proves this fact. Both sides make mistakes, and the cost in human lives is high. For Andrew, this is another kind of disillusionment—the men whom he most respected fell short in upholding their duties. Worse yet, they fail to even understand situations like Tushin's. Nicholas, too, did not find the experience to be anything like he had expected.

Key Takeaways:

"'No, friend,' said a pleasant and, as it seemed to Prince Andrew, a familiar voice, 'what I say is that if it were possible to know what is beyond death, none of us would be afraid of it. That's so, friend.'" Captain Tushin expresses Tolstoy's own thoughts about death at the time (his views continued to change over the course of his long life). Nicholas is outwardly afraid of death, and even the thrill of being alive that Andrew feels in battle is a product of this same fear of death and the unknown. Humble Captain Tushin is the first of a series of wise, eccentric characters who impart deep truths.

"'Who are they? Why are they running? Can they be coming at me? And why? To kill me? Me whom everyone is so fond of?' He remembered his mother's love for him, and his family's, and his friends', and the enemy's intention to kill him seemed impossible. 'But perhaps they may do it!'" In one of the most poignant scenes in the novel, Nicholas (who is around 18 years old) gallops into battle and is immediately wounded, his horse is killed, and he finds himself alone. He wonders whether he is dead. No one helps him—he has to save himself, first running off the field, then begging for a ride on a wagon, then lying delirious back at camp.

BOOK THREE

1805

Book 3: Chapters 1-5

What Happens?

Back in Moscow, since Pierre unexpectedly inherited his father's title and much of his wealth, he is now sought after in society and considered an extremely eligible bachelor. Prince Vasili Kuragin attaches himself to Pierre, ostensibly "helping" him with business affairs. Really, though, he is doing everything possible to encourage him to fall in love with his daughter, Helene.

When Pierre goes to Petersburg, Anna Pavlovna Scherer helps in this endeavor, so that Pierre and Helene are almost always thrown together in social situations. Despite his serious reservations, he continues to spend time with the Kuragins. Growing impatient, Vasili throws a name-day party for Helene. At the end of the evening, he walks into the room where Pierre and Helene, who have not yet spoken of love, are sitting, and congratulates them on their engagement. Everyone goes along with this announcement, and six weeks later, they are married. Now Vasili can concentrate on the other marriage he wishes to arrange: that of his son, Anatole, and Mary Bolkonskaya. He sends word to Prince Nicholas Bolkonski that he is coming to visit.

The elderly prince is in a bad mood because he realizes what Vasili is planning. He orders that the snow that was just plowed out of the road now be plowed back into it. Lise and Mademoiselle Bourienne try to arrange Mary's clothing and hair to best advantage, but end up making her look worse—and even more frightened and unhappy than usual. The three women are all captivated by the handsome, quiet Anatole, though each with different intentions—Mary with thoughts of being his wife, Mlle. Bourienne plans to let him seduce her, and Lise wants to flirt with him, since coquetry is second nature for her. In the morning, Bolkonski tells his daughter he will let her make her own choice, but he points out to her that Anatole clearly is interested in Mlle. Bourienne. Mary finds the two kissing, and ends up comforting her friend. She refuses the proposed marriage with dignity, finally coming into her own as a Bolkonski.

Analysis:

The two scenes of aggressive matchmaking by Prince Vasili are placed in parallel, showing the differences in character between Pierre and Mary. While being in some ways similar—both characters were raised in relative isolation, and have little experience with ruthless fortune hunters, yet both possess fortunes—they have different natures. Pierre has to experience life firsthand, learning only from his own mistakes, while Mary has a strong moral core that enables her to avoid disaster. Pierre, of course, is only twenty years old, and with his father gone and Andrew at the war front, he has no one to guide him. Mary, for better or worse, has her father to deter dangerous people (using actual snow, when necessary).

Key Takeaways:

"*Formerly in Anna Pavlovna's presence, Pierre had always felt that what he was saying was out of place, tactless and unsuitable, that remarks which seemed to him clever while they formed in his mind became foolish as soon as he uttered them, while on the contrary Hippolyte's stupidest remarks came out clever and apt. Now everything Pierre said was charmant.*" Mary's prediction in her letter to Julie Karagina turned out to be correct: Pierre's fortune would be more of a burden than a blessing for him. He truly loses his head, being surrounded by so much flattery and kindness, after having so long been merely tolerated in society.

"'*But she's stupid. I have myself said she is stupid,*' he thought. '*There is something nasty, something wrong, in the feeling she excites in me. I have been told that her brother Anatole was in love with her and she with him, that there was quite a scandal and that's why he was sent away. Hippolyte is her brother... Prince Vasili is her father... It's bad...*' he reflected, but while he was thinking this (the reflection was still incomplete), he caught himself smiling.*" Pierre is weak, and does not know how to extricate himself from the web Vasili has created for him. Mary, on the other hand, acknowledges that she is weak, and does not allow herself to end up in the power of these strangers.

"'*Prince Vasili finds you to his taste as a daughter-in-law and makes a proposal to you on his pupil's behalf. That's how it's to be understood!*'" Prince Nicholas is remarkably insightful about other people. He sees that Vasili is the mastermind of this scheme, and Anatole is his "pupil"—like his father, he will make a career of using other people.

Book 3: Chapters 6-8

What Happens?

The Rostov family is distraught when a letter arrives with news of the battle in which Nicholas participated and was injured (but subsequently promoted). Sonya is devastated to hear Nicholas has been hurt, while Natasha has started to forget what Boris looks like. The family members write letters to Nicholas, and send six thousand rubles.

Now stationed near Olmutz, Boris ensures that the money gets to Nicholas, and they spend some time together with Lieutenant Berg, Vera's soon-to-be fiancé. Nicholas embellishes on the facts of the battle to them, but he is contradicted by Andrew, who has just come in. Nicholas rudely implies that Andrew is the kind of military man who earns medals without ever seeing combat. Andrew instantly dislikes Nicholas, and though the latter is angry, on reflection he realizes that he would like to have the older man as his friend.

Then Emperor Alexander comes to inspect the troops, and Nicholas is struck with hero worship. He is completely swept up in the moment, and is angry when he sees Andrew sitting on his horse carelessly, unmoved. The Emperor's visit has encouraged most of the troops, though—they are eager to go into battle.

Analysis:

The scene with Nicholas retelling the battle scene is important, because Nicholas is doing what Tolstoy himself is doing—telling the story of a war. In Nicholas' account, the facts are replaced by dramatic clichés. He is telling his audience the story they want to hear, and the story that reflects nothing bad upon himself or his friends. Historians fall into both of those traps as they write history; Tolstoy wants to be the first to tell the stories without clichés, embellishments, or intentional omissions.

Key Takeaways:

"'It is some letter of recommendation... what the devil do I want it for!'

' Why "What the devil"? said Boris, picking it up and reading the address. 'This letter would be of great use to you.'

'I want nothing, and I won't be anyone's adjutant.'

'Why not?' inquired Boris.

'It's a lackey's job!'"

Boris's mother had procured the letter for Nicholas, instead of her own son, and he shows no appreciation for that fact, or that his family is thinking of his safety after hearing of his injury. Boris, meanwhile, will have to continue to make his own way.

"He told them of his Schon Grabern affair, just as those who have taken part in a battle generally do describe it, that is, as they would like it to have been, as they have heard it described by others, and as sounds well, but not at all as it really was." Tolstoy presents a fictional commentary on the nature of history and the shortcomings of historians. Nicholas falls into this pattern of telling what he wishes had happened, but Andrew, who cares little about others' opinions of him, and who has been disappointed in his high hopes for this war, can tell the truth.

Book 3: Chapters 9-19

What Happens?

Boris asks Andrew to help him get promoted to adjutant. Andrew takes him to Prince Dolgorukov, keeping himself within the circle of favors while not asking them for his own benefit. This visit does not result in much for Boris, since all are occupied with the upcoming battle, but he has begun learning how the diplomatic world works, "the unwritten code" which allows men to rise up in rank.

Sidelined for a time while other regiments capture a French squadron, the Pavlograd hussars are in low spirits until the Emperor passes by them on his way to see the battle. He looks directly at Nicholas, fueling the latter's adoration and prompting a night of toasting the Emperor's health. Alexander, meanwhile, is so distressed at seeing the dead and wounded soldiers that he is ill the following day. Napoleon's envoy arrives, asking for a peace treaty. Prince Dolgorukov goes to meet with Napoleon, but no agreement is reached.

The night before the battle, the German general, Weyrother, proposes a plan to attack the French. Andrew has developed an alternate plan, but no one pays attention to him. Kutuzov believes they will be defeated, but his concerns fall on deaf ears as well. Andrew realizes that tens of thousands of lives may be lost the following day, including his own. Fatalistically, he decides to give his all in the battle, to win glory for himself even if he dies. Meanwhile, Nicholas Rostov is patrolling the borders of the camp that night. He sleepily jumbles together thoughts of the Emperor, his assignment, and memories of home in Moscow. Suddenly, shouting begins in the French camp. As Nicholas rides closer to investigate, someone shoots at him. It turns out that the shouting was in response to Napoleon's encouragement to fight bravely the next day.

At daybreak, the Russian troops advance into the foggy valley. There are miscommunications, miscalculations, and bad weather, so that Napoleon is actually watching as the Russians take their positions. The French troops are much closer than anticipated, and Kutuzov seems to be the only one who understands that the troop formations must be changed to accommodate this. The enemy attacks, and some Russian soldiers run away in fear. The standard bearer (the soldier who carries the flag showing the troops where to go) is killed, so Andrew picks it up and calls the soldiers to follow him. They obey, but before long Andrew is wounded.

Meanwhile, Prince Bagration does not want to take responsibility for sending troops into battle, so he stalls by sending Nicholas as a messenger to ask Kutuzov or the Emperor what to do. He is nearly trampled by a cavalry charge, and then comes under cannon fire (the Russians and Austrians are actually firing at one another). Kutuzov is nowhere to be found as Nicholas rides through fields strewn with casualties. He finds Emperor Alexander alone in one such field, but is too shy to approach him. By five o'clock the battle has been lost on all points. In one gruesome scene, Dolokhov's regiment jumps onto an icy pond to escape cannon fire, only to drown when the ice breaks. After the fighting has ended, Napoleon himself tours the battlefield and finds Andrew alive. The Russian officers are taken prisoner, but the fatally wounded are left to the care of the local people.

Analysis:

The story of the battle is told through the eyes of Andrew and Nicholas, both of whom seek to find the approval of others through their actions on the battlefield. Nicholas wants to distinguish himself in front of the Emperor, who has an amazing ability to influence the troops to fight—even though, it seems, he has no stomach for war. Rostov would willingly die in front of the Emperor, yet he is afraid to have a practical conversation with him. On the other hand, Andrew denies to himself that he wants this approval, making himself even more miserable for it. He is intellectually sophisticated (no doubt thanks in part to his father's tutelage), but emotionally repressed (also part of his father's influence). As he lies near death on the battlefield, staring up at the infinite sky as if for the first time, he realizes he loves his father, his sister, his wife, and his future son. He meets his hero, Napoleon, but whose words are like "The buzzing of a fly," insignificant in comparison with his lofty thoughts of life and death. He wants to be brought back to life now that he finally understands it.

Key Takeaways:

"Just as in the mechanism of a clock, so in the mechanism of the military machine, an impulse once given leads to the final result; and just as indifferently quiescent till the moment when motion is transmitted to them are the parts of the mechanism which the impulse has not yet reached. Wheels creak on their axles as the cogs engage one another and the revolving pulleys whirr with the rapidity of their movement, but a neighboring wheel is as quiet and motionless as though it were prepared to remain so for a hundred years; but the moment comes when the lever catches it and obeying the impulse that wheel begins to creak and joins in the common motion the result and aim of which are beyond its ken." The battle of Austerlitz illustrates how many different smaller circumstances, decisions, and accidents shape the greater course of history. The ever-wise General Kutuzov knows that the battle will be catastrophic, but cannot turn back the other men who are so determined to fight.

"So insignificant at that moment seemed to him all the interests that engrossed Napoleon, so mean did his hero himself with his paltry vanity and joy in victory appear, compared to the lofty, equitable, and kindly sky which he had seen and understood, that he could not answer him.

"Everything seemed so futile and insignificant in comparison with the stern and solemn train of thought that weakness from loss of blood, suffering, and the nearness of death aroused in him. Looking into Napoleon's eyes Prince Andrew thought of the insignificance of greatness, the unimportance of life which no one could understand, and the still greater unimportance of death, the meaning of which no one alive could understand or explain." Just as Nicholas has his moment of disappointment with his hero, Emperor Alexander, so too Andrew looks into Napoleon's eyes and declines to speak with him. The latter's indifference to death (and thus lack of appreciation for life) render him insignificant in the world that has opened up to Andrew.

BOOK FOUR

1806

Book 4: Chapters 1-6

What Happens?

Nicholas Rostov returns home on leave, bringing his friend Denisov. The household is ecstatic to see him after a year and a half. Natasha tells Nicholas that Sonya still loves him but releases him from their secret engagement. He is relieved because he wants to remain free for a while longer.

Count Ilya Rostov has remortgaged his estates in order to finance the family's busy social schedule, including throwing a banquet in honor of Prince Bagration. Pierre is invited; unfortunately, so is Dolokhov, who has, it is rumored, been having an affair with Pierre's wife, Helene. Dolokhov behaves in a cruel, mocking manner to Pierre, who impulsively challenges him to a duel.

Denisov, Rostov, and Nesvitski are present for the duel, and each in turn tries to talk the men out of it, to no avail. Amazingly, though Pierre has never held a pistol before, he wounds his rival. Nicholas and Denisov take Dolokhov home, and the arrogant, debauched bully starts to cry for his mother's sake: it turns out that he is absolutely devoted to his aged mother and his hunchbacked sister.

Pierre is convinced that Dolokhov will die and he will be a murderer. He goes home, and in a heated argument, Helene shows her contempt for him as she denies the infidelity. Pierre separates from her, giving her over half his fortune.

Analysis:

While his friends have been on the battlefield, Pierre has been at war within himself. He realizes that he never loved his wife, and never felt right in saying so, but at the same time it bolstered his pride to be married to such an admired woman. As they argue, he becomes so angry he throws a marble tabletop at her. With these two acts of violence against Dolokhov and Helene, he severs ties with the life he has been leading, and must start another stage of his journey.

Key Takeaways:

"Reasons were found for the incredible, unheard-of, and impossible event of a Russian defeat, everything became clear, and in all corners of Moscow the same things began to be said. These reasons were the treachery of the Austrians, a defective commissariat... Kutuzov's incapacity, and (it was whispered) the youth and inexperience of the sovereign, who had trusted worthless and insignificant people. But the army, the Russian army, everyone declared, was extraordinary and had achieved miracles of valor. The soldiers, officers, and generals were heroes. But the hero of heroes was Prince Bagration... What also conduced to Bagration's being selected as Moscow's hero was the fact that he had no connections in the city and was a stranger there." In one of Tolstoy's most cynical passages, he lambastes Moscow society, first for not appreciating his beloved Kutuzov, and second, for having such a tightly woven web of criticism and gossip that only an outsider can be appreciated there.

"'You know, Count, it is much more honorable to admit one's mistake than to let matters become irreparable. There was no insult on either side. Allow me to convey...'

'No! What is there to talk about?' said Pierre. 'It's all the same... Is everything ready?'" With his acceptance of the rumor of his wife's infidelity after a few short months of marriage, Pierre has become fatalistic in his outlook, much the same way Andrew had. He is taking out his anger at himself, Helene and Prince Vasili on Dolokhov.

Book 4: Chapters 7-9

What Happens?

Two months have passed since the battle of Austerlitz, and there has been no news of Andrew. His body was not found on the battlefield, nor was his name on the list of prisoners. At Bald Hills, the old prince believes his son to be dead, while Mary holds hope that he is alive, but neither one of them is able to speak of the situation at all to Lise, who is soon to give birth.

In March, Lise goes into labor, and the Bolkonskis send for both a midwife and a doctor. A carriage arrives bringing not only the doctor, but Andrew as well. He hears Lise in agony and runs into the room, but she barely seems to acknowledge him. She has a childlike, reproachful expression on her face.

Andrew is sent out of the room by the midwife, and hears terrible screaming and finally a baby crying. The baby is healthy, but Lise has died—with that same expression on her face. The child is named after his grandfather, who also serves as his godfather.

Analysis:

Lise lived a shallow life of leisure, attending parties, and flirting, which makes her death all the more tragic—she never really lived. Andrew took her out of her comfortable world and abandoned her in a strange, anxiety-filled place, exacerbating the riskiness of pregnancy. Their marriage ruined both of their lives, and ended Lise's. The same story is told with several variations in *War and Peace*: when two people are mismatched in character, their relationship can only damage them.

The scene, like the earlier death scene of Count Bezukhov, is also a meditation on the interconnectedness of life and death, joy and sorrow. In almost the same moment, Andrew feels overjoyed that his son has been born, but also sadness and guilt at the death of his wife.

Key Takeaways:

"But owing to the superstition that the fewer the people who know of it the less a woman in travail suffers, everyone tried to pretend not to know; no one spoke of it, but apart from the ordinary staid and respectful good manners habitual in the prince's household, a common anxiety, a softening of the heart, and a consciousness that something great and mysterious was being accomplished at that moment made itself felt." In a touching scene, the whole household shares in the anticipation of the baby's arrival, including the servants. The old prince's mathematical, structured ways are temporarily superseded by the supernatural—the answered prayer of Andrew's return home, and the superstitions of pretending not to know of the woman in labor, and later the lucky sign at the baptism, when the infant's hair, cut by the priest as part of the ceremony, is placed in wax and floats (it is bad luck if it sinks).

"And there in the coffin was the same face, though with closed eyes. 'Ah, what have you done to me?' it still seemed to say, and Prince Andrew felt that something gave way in his soul and that he was guilty of a sin he could neither remedy nor forget." Lise, the "little princess," was intimidated by her husband and afraid of her father-in-law, but in death she asserts power over them both—the reproachful look on her face strikes both of them with guilt and remorse. The reproachful words she spoke to Andrew at their home in Petersburg months before are echoed here, and will continue to haunt Andrew.

Book 4: Chapters 10-16

What Happens?

In Moscow, Dolokhov recovers from his wound from the duel. He and Nicholas Rostov become good friends. The Rostov family grows fond of Dolokhov, with the exception of Natasha, who distrusts him. Dolokhov develops an interest in Sonya that is apparent to all the family, and finally he asks for her hand in marriage, but she refuses. She is still in love with Nicholas, though she tells him (as he pleads with her to reconsider Dolokhov's offer) that she loves him like a brother. By the autumn of 1806, it is clear that Nicholas and Denisov will be called back to duty—Napoleon is escalating the conflict once again.

Meanwhile, Denisov falls in love with Natasha, with whom he dances at a ball. About to rejoin his regiment, Dolokhov invites Nicholas to a card game at his hotel, a game that confirms the rumors that Dolokhov is a card sharp in addition to his other faults. Nicholas loses all his money and more—the final sum he owes is forty-three thousand rubles. Nicholas promises to pay the money back the next day, and returns home in shame and despair. He asks his father for the money, but it takes the count two weeks to raise it.

At the very same moment, in another room, Denisov proposes to Natasha, but she too rejects his offer. Her mother is angry that he would make an offer of marriage to such a young girl without even speaking to her parents, and Denisov is mortified. The happy times that the young people enjoyed are over, and Denisov and Nicholas leave Moscow.

Analysis:

Tolstoy does not arrange chapters in chronological order, but instead places them in logical juxtapositions. After the previous scenes at Bald Hills, where the prevailing spirit of the house was so austere and oppressive that it seems partly to blame in Lise's death, we now see the polar opposite in the Rostovs' home, where love and kindness reign. Outsiders feel not only welcome but drawn there, as Denisov and Dolokhov both experience. Even when Nicholas goes to his father to confess his costly mistake, his father shows no anger, only understanding and comfort.

At the beginning of these chapters, Nicholas still seems like a spoiled child of privilege. His father hushes up his part in the duel, and he gets a prestigious job as adjutant (even though he had earlier said it was a lackey's job). Ironically, Dolokhov's mother complains to Nicholas that Pierre has repeatedly escaped punishment for his bad behavior because he is rich, even though her son benefited from the Rostovs' connections hushing up the duel the same way. The loss of the forty-three thousand rubles, though, will be the catalyst for Nicholas' journey to adulthood.

Key Takeaways:

"Never had love been so much in the air, and never had the amorous atmosphere made itself so strongly felt in the Rostovs' house as at this holiday time. 'Seize the moments of happiness, love and be loved! That is the only reality in the world, all else is folly. It is the one thing we are interested in here,' said the spirit of the place." As future chapters will develop, the Rostov family possesses intangible qualities that other families in the story seem to lack. Instinctively, though they are as cultured and Europeanized as the rest of the elite society, they feel more deeply and impulsively, and care more about others—they are truly what it means (to Tolstoy) to be Russian.

"And without noticing that he was singing, to strengthen the si he sung a second, a third below the high note. 'Ah, God! How fine! Did I really take it? How fortunate!' he thought. Oh, how that chord vibrated, and how moved was something that was finest in Rostov's soul! And this something was apart from everything else in the world and above everything in the world. 'What were losses, and Dolokhov, and words of honor?... All nonsense! One might kill and rob and yet be happy...'" Here Nicholas begins to harmonize with Natasha, almost without realizing he is even singing. The siblings, despite their growing up and the long time spent apart, still maintain their close bond, and as Natasha conveys pure feeling with her voice, it helps to lift Nicholas from the depths of despair.

BOOK FIVE

1806-1807

Book 5: Chapters 1-5

What Happens?

While en route to Petersburg, and in an unhappy state of mind, Pierre is approached by a mysterious stranger, who knows all about him and his misfortunes. Pierre recognizes that the man is a Freemason, whose beliefs he normally derides. He confesses to the man that he is an atheist, and they have a lengthy discussion about the possible natures of God. The stranger advises Pierre that he needs to seek God, to comprehend him not with reason but with the inner self, which needs to be purified.

The stranger, whose name turns out to be Joseph Alexeevich Bazdeev, invites Pierre to join the brotherhood of Freemasons when he arrives in Petersburg. He does, finding hope and optimism about the future for the first time in many months. After a long initiation ceremony during which even the members seem to get a little confused, Pierre confesses that his primary vice is women, and sets out to improve himself in this regard.

The next day, after he is admitted into the lodge, his father-in-law appears, trying in his usual way to coerce Pierre, this time to take Helene back. Now that he is a new man with ambitious dreams, Pierre finds it easy to send him away, much to Vasili's surprise. Pierre departs for his estates in the south.

Analysis:

Perhaps only Tolstoy would insert a *deus ex machina* moment in which a character is brought to have faith in a deity via a long and rather dull digression into Masonic initiation. Still, we see the masterfulness of Tolstoy's character development, in that his characters are never static, even when there is relatively less plot action. At this time in between wars, both Pierre and Andrew are undergoing deep spiritual changes. Typical for Pierre, the next chapter of his life will be determined by his connection with others.

Key Takeaways:

"No matter what he thought about, he always returned to these

same questions which he could not solve and yet could not cease to ask himself. It was as if the thread of the chief screw which held his life together were stripped, so that the screw could not get in or out, but went on turning uselessly in the same place." At this point in the novel, all three of our main male characters are in crises. This marvelous image of a screw spinning uselessly perfectly describes the state in which Pierre finds himself, and shows how inevitable it is that he will make a change, though it is another unwise one.

"When everything was ready, the stranger opened his eyes, moved to the table, filled a tumbler with tea for himself and one for the beardless old man to whom he passed it. Pierre began to feel a sense of uneasiness, and the need, even the inevitability, of entering into conversation with this stranger." While most of the many characters in *War and Peace* are ordinary people—and some of them actual historical figures—Tolstoy does insert a handful of mystical, fairy-tale-like characters, of which this mysterious old man and his servant are two. The master pours tea for his servant, suggesting equality between them.

Book 5: Chapters 6-7

What Happens?

Anna Pavlovna Scherer holds another one of her soirees. As usual, the conversation consists of gossip and politics. Although Count Rostov had the duel hushed up so that no criminal charges were brought against the participants, everyone knows about it. They feel that Pierre has treated Dolokhov and Helene badly.

The political conversation has not changed from the year before—everyone hates Napoleon as much as ever. Hippolyte Kuragin draws all attention to himself, as usual, making jokes about the war. Boris Drubetskoy, who has been ambitiously working his way up in society, is the arranged entertainment for the evening, reporting on his trip to Prussia. He is a born diplomat, careful not to insert his opinions.

Boris meets Helene Bezukhova, who is still the darling of the social circle. She insists that he visit her at her home. He soon becomes a regular guest there.

Analysis:

After a long digression into faith and mysticism, we return once again to the vacuous drawing room at Anna Pavlovna's. While Pierre is genuinely trying to improve his mind and heart, the general opinion is that he is a jealous, violent fool, and that Helene is a martyr to be married to such a monster. Interestingly, it is still unclear whether Helene actually had an affair with Dolokhov, but it does not really matter anymore—the marriage would have fallen apart in any case. Now, however, she seems quite intent on making Boris her lover.

Key Takeaways:

"The remembrance of the Rostovs' house and of his childish love for Natasha was unpleasant to him and he had not once been to see the Rostovs since the day of his departure for the army. To be in Anna Pavlovna's drawing room he considered an important step up in the service, and he at once understood his role, letting his hostess make use of whatever interest he had to offer. He himself carefully scanned each face, appraising the possibilities of establishing intimacy with each of those present, and the advantages that might accrue." Although he lived with the Rostovs instead of his mother, and was educated by them (not to mention the financial support they gave), now that they are declining in wealth, he wants nothing more to do with them. He is voluntarily cutting himself off from this loving environment in order to pursue his own advantages. It seems he, unlike Pierre and Andrew, is the kind of man for whom a shallow, vapid woman will suffice; he and Helene might deserve each other.

Book 5: Chapters 8-14

What Happens?

At Bald Hills, the old prince, though weakened by age and the stress of the previous year, agrees to oversee the military recruitment in the area. Mary and Mlle. Bourienne are caring for the baby. Andrew takes charge of the nearby estate his father gave to him, called Bogucharovo, and is trying to avoid involvement in military affairs. His father and Bilibin send him the latest news of war. The latter's sardonic descriptions of the petty foibles of the key players in the war are, Andrew knows, most likely exaggerated, but still they upset him. In any case, he is determined to remain at home and care for his child.

Meanwhile, Pierre, too, is working on his estates. Thanks to his new beliefs, he wants to free his serfs, build hospitals and schools, and set up other such good works; however, his total lack of business sense means that his stewards and foremen are cheating him at every turn, and his proposed projects would only add to the burden of the already overworked peasants. Imagining he has done good works on his journey, Pierre is in a happy state of mind and decides to visit Andrew on his way home.

The pair has not met in two years, and both have changed greatly. Andrew is thinner, older, and despondent. Pierre has, of course, made a mess of his life with the marriage, the duel, and now these lofty plans and new philosophies. Pierre works up the courage to tell Andrew that the source of his newfound hope for the future is Freemasonry, and, to his surprise, his friend does not scoff. Lise's death has left him with questions for which he feels there must be an answer. Looking at the night sky, he remembers the sight of the "infinite sky" above the battleground at Austerlitz.

Andrew and Pierre drive to Bald Hills, where Mary is receiving some holy pilgrims, against her father's wishes. Andrew and Pierre gently ridicule the stories told by the people, and Mary chastises them. After they leave, Pierre starts to feel remorse for his teasing. Old Prince Bolkonski returns home and enjoys debating with Pierre. The whole family is fond of him.

Analysis:

These chapters provide a panorama of how individuals search for meaning. Andrew and Pierre have settled into opposite priorities—Andrew living for himself and his son, Pierre trying to live for everyone else—but they are surrounded by other examples as well. Andrew's father has come back to life in his new job—but for as much energy and strategy as he brings to the war effort, he also wants too much power over others. Mary has devoted herself to her family and her faith, but the anger that so often rises in her suggests that she is not fulfilled in the current state of her life. The religious pilgrims have devoted themselves to selfless living, and so fear neither death nor changes in life.

Key Takeaways:

"The old prince and his son seemed to have changed roles since the campaign of 1805. The old man, roused by activity, expected the best results from the new campaign, while Prince Andrew on the contrary, taking no part in the war and secretly regretting this, saw only the dark side." Although the campaign of 1805 was devastating to the country and to the Bolkonskis personally, the old prince has ideas for how to make a success of it in 1807— and so does Andrew, though he tries to suppress them.

"'I only know two very real evils in life: remorse and illness. The only good is the absence of those evils. To live for myself avoiding those two evils is my whole philosophy now.'" Andrew enjoys arguing with Pierre (that is one thing that has not changed about him), but even as he declares that it is enough to live for one's own interests, he and Pierre are both aware of how deeply unhappy he is.

Book 5: Chapters 15-22

What Happens?

Now in Poland, Nicholas Rostov is happy to be serving in his regiment, far away from the concerns of love and debt back home. He is determined to live in poverty and pay back his debt to his father. There is no food for the soldiers in the ruined village where they are encamped—or anyone else for that matter. The soldiers eat wild plants, and feed their horses straw from the roofs of cottages. Nicholas has the generous Rostov nature—he begins secretly taking care of a Polish family.

Denisov, desperate to provide for his hungry men, commandeers provisions from a wagon that was intended for the infantry. He is called to account for this, and learns that Telyanin, the man who stole his purse, has been holding back supplies from the Pavlograd hussars. Denisov is going to be court-martialed. In the next fight, he suffers a minor flesh wound and goes to the infirmary. Rostov visits him there, and before he finds the officers' ward, he experiences the nightmarish sights and smells of the soldiers' ward. When he gets to the relatively comfortable officers' ward, he meets Captain Tushin, who has had an arm amputated. Denisov gives Nicholas a petition to take to the Emperor.

Nicholas goes to Tilsit, where Alexander I and Napoleon are meeting to negotiate peace. Boris Drubetskoy is there, though he is not glad to see Nicholas. He does, however, offer the advice that Nicholas should give Denisov's letter to an army commander, rather than directly to the Emperor. Nicholas tries anyway, and ends up giving it to an acquaintance, a general who sympathizes with Denisov's case. He talks of the matter to the Emperor, who refuses to intervene. Nicholas is further troubled when the Emperors exchange medals and sign the treaty, and Napoleon awards a medal to a soldier selected almost at random. The injustices he has seen raise questions that would shake his deepest convictions, so he chooses to bury them, to drink, and to keep obeying.

Analysis:

Nicholas Rostov is a different sort of person than Andrew and Pierre—he requires little to be content, and he is not so prone to introspection. Normally he has little trouble reconciling the needs of the individual with the greater good. This time, however, he sees so many injustices in such a short period of time that he cannot help but start questioning. The fact that a starving man took food to give to other starving men does not seem to merit the punishment of court-martial and demotion. The friend who was raised with him like a brother is now barely civil to him. The squalid, disease-filled hospital stands in sharp contrast to the lavish ceremonies for the Emperors at Tilsit. The Emperor whom he so admired not only rudely dismisses his petition, but he treats the "upstart" Emperor, Napoleon, as an equal, even though Alexander was born into the monarchy. At the end of the day, though, he has to hold to the same code that Alexander cited—the law is mightier than any individual, even the Emperor. Nicholas is determined to stay his course.

Key Takeaways:

"[When] the officers collected round to greet the new arrival, Rostov experienced the same feeling as when his mother, his father, and his sister had embraced him, and tears of joy choked him so that he could not speak. The regiment was also a home, and as unalterably dear and precious as his parents' house." The line between war and peace has become incredibly blurred for Nicholas. He receives the same welcome at the regiment that he does at home. After his initial experiences of panic on the battlefield, he has grown accustomed to it, and the social world of the military is preferable to the society back home, which has no check and balances.

"'You are speaking of Buonaparte?' asked the general, smiling.

Boris looked at his general inquiringly and immediately saw that he was being tested.

'I am speaking, Prince, of the Emperor Napoleon,' he replied. The general patted him on the shoulder, with a smile.

'You will go far,' he said, and took him to Tilsit with him." In contrast to Nicholas, Pierre, and Andrew, who are all so honest that they can sometimes seem impolite and not tactful, Boris is a born diplomat. We have seen the desperation of his circumstances—he and his mother are very poor, despite still belonging to aristocratic circles—so we can understand why he has to ingratiate himself with powerful people. At the same time, the fact that he does so at the expense of his friendships with others who are not in a position to help him suggests that his character is lacking the finer qualities that the other young men in the novel possess.

"Life meanwhile—real life, with its essential interests of health and sickness, toil and rest, and its intellectual interests in thought, science, poetry, music, love, friendship, hatred, and passions—went on as usual, independently of and apart from political friendship or enmity with Napoleon Bonaparte and from all the schemes of reconstruction." Tolstoy concludes Book Five with a chapter composed entirely of editorial commentary. This device will appear more and more frequently as the book progresses. The idea expressed here, that ordinary life continued its course without being affected by Napoleon and Alexander, will be illustrated by the events in Book Six.

BOOK SIX

1808-1810

Book 6: Chapters 1-6

What Happens?

Prince Andrew has been successful in managing his estates, and undertaking the kind of reforms at which Pierre had been unsuccessful. In the spring of 1809, Andrew visits the Rostovs at their country estate, Otradnoe, while tending to some issues of his own estate. Andrew is puzzled at how Natasha can be so exuberantly happy. As he returns home, he begins to feel that his life is not over after all.

Andrew goes to Petersburg in the autumn of 1809 to present his ideas for army reform to the Emperor. He is sent to meet with the Minister of War, Count Arakcheev. The count does not approve his plan, but offers him an unpaid job on the Committee of Army Regulations.

Andrew is accepted back into Petersburg society, and has many social engagements. Finally, he meets Michael Speranski, the youthful Secretary of State who has a great deal of influence over the Emperor. There is a mutual respect between the two, and Andrew finds himself becoming involved in the war effort once more.

Analysis:

Proving Tolstoy's assertion at the end of Book Five, Andrew's involvement with the war effort (necessitated by Napoleon's actions) will ultimately not make him happy; his springtime rebirth and growing attraction to Natasha will—and these would have happened even if no war had been taking place in Europe.

With his estate reforms, including liberating his serfs and educating peasant children, Andrew is decades ahead of his time. Russian society began seriously debating the abolition of serfdom in the 1840s, and finally Tsar Alexander II (grandson of the Alexander in *War and Peace*) officially freed all serfs in 1861. Literacy among the lower classes of society was very low until the Soviet era.

Key Takeaways:

Andrew sees a lone oak tree which has not yet begun to blossom as all the other species of trees have, though it is a larger and stronger tree than the rest of the forest. He imagines this tree speaking as if it were his incarnation in the plant world, the one hopeless pessimist who cannot be excited about the future. He decides he cannot start anything new, but rather must live out his life as it is now. After visiting the Rostovs, though, he sees the oak again, now covered in foliage.

"*To Bolkonski so many people appeared contemptible and insignificant creatures, and he so longed to find in someone the living ideal of that perfection toward which he strove, that he readily believed that in Speranski he had found this ideal of a perfectly rational and virtuous man. Had Speranski sprung from the same class as himself and possessed the same breeding and traditions, Bolkonski would soon have discovered his weak, human, unheroic sides; but as it was, Speranski's strange and logical turn of mind inspired him with respect all the more because he did not quite understand him. Moreover, Speranski, either because he appreciated the other's capacity or because he considered it necessary to win him to his side, showed off his dispassionate calm reasonableness before Prince Andrew and flattered him with that subtle flattery which goes hand in hand with self-assurance and consists in a tacit assumption that one's companion is the only man besides oneself capable of understanding the folly of the rest of mankind and the reasonableness and profundity of one's own ideas.*" Andrew's friendship with Speranski will challenge his long-held beliefs and prejudices about class, money, nobility, and the worth of other human beings.

Book 6: Chapters 7-10

What Happens?

The story returns to Pierre, in Petersburg, starting in 1808. He keeps busy with his duties among the Petersburg Freemasons, and becomes one of the most prominent and generous members. At the same time, though, he stays involved with the same vices as before. He is also bothered by the hypocrisy of many of the members in Russia. He decides to go abroad to be initiated into the "Higher secrets of the order."

He returns in the summer of 1809 and makes a speech based on his new ideas for how the Freemasons around the world could unite to solve their problems. Half of the members receive it with enthusiasm, and the rest accuse him of radical thoughts. The Grand Master of the lodge says that something negative in his nature must have made him want to cause strife among the Brothers. Pierre becomes disillusioned with Freemasonry.

Around the same time, Helene writes to him, begging for reconciliation. He visits his mentor Joseph Bazdeev, who is very ill, and the latter reprimands him for the speech he gave. In a state of depression, he resumes living with his wife, though he maintains his distance from her. Helene wastes no time in establishing herself in society as a great hostess, and, more astonishingly, as a witty, clever woman. Boris Drubetskoy is a close friend of Helene's, and Pierre feels a strong aversion toward Boris, whom he had once liked. Nonetheless, he sponsors Boris for membership in the Freemasons.

Analysis:

Just as Andrew has become involved in a government job that will fall short of his hopes, and has become friends with someone who will not help him on his spiritual journey, Pierre, too, is finding that the human organization in which he has invested so much falls far short of meeting his needs (and the needs of others). He has become a leader of the Petersburg Freemasons, not because of any particular ambition to be such, but because he is generous with his funds while other members give very little, and because he is sincerely committed to improving the lives of others. Pierre never seems to succeed in this latter goal. Also, he still lacks strong willpower and has never truly given up his old habits of drinking (and, Tolstoy hints very delicately, of visiting brothels). At the same time, though, he is tormented by the idea that he should resume marital relations with his wife, although he does not love or respect her.

Key Takeaways:

For the first time, it is mentioned that Pierre keeps a diary. This allows the reader full access into Pierre's thoughts, and the diary itself is a kind of symbol for Pierre's life—he leaves pages blank to indicate when things are happening that are not described in his diary or in the novel. He records his dreams, which are full of details he tries to interpret; for instance, after a tiff with Boris, he dreams of being attacked by dogs, which he thinks symbolizes how his passions are out of control.

"I got up late. On waking I lay long in bed yielding to sloth. O God, help and strengthen me that I may walk in Thy ways! Read the Scriptures, but without proper feeling." Pierre is brutally honest and detailed in his diary, and the result is almost comical, though probably not intentionally so on Tolstoy's part.

Book 6: Chapters 11-17

What Happens?

Although living in the country, the Rostovs are still living beyond their means. The count takes the family to Petersburg as he looks for employment, and so that his family may enjoy themselves for what may be the last time. The oldest daughter, Vera, becomes engaged to a German officer, Berg. The estate that was to have been her dowry has been sold, and Count Rostov must raise money instead.

Having been childhood sweethearts, Natasha and Boris finally renew their acquaintance in Petersburg. The ever-ambitious Boris knows that he must marry well, and that Helene Bezukhova is jealous of anyone else having his attention, but still he cannot help but visit the Rostovs daily. Natasha's mother knows that her daughter is not in love with Boris, and that he is an unsuitable match for her, so she tells him not to visit so often.

The Rostovs are invited to a grand ball on New Year's Eve of 1810—the first Natasha has ever attended. They spend all day getting ready, and finally arrive late—but the Emperor arrives later still. Countess Rostova's friend Marya Ignatevna Peronskaya attends with them and points out all the important Petersburg people. The dancing begins and Natasha wants to cry as no one asks her to dance at first. Pierre requests that Andrew ask Natasha to dance, and Andrew is charmed and rejuvenated by her.

Analysis:

Despite its great length, *War and Peace* has some famous, highly acclaimed chapters, and these are among them. It is truly marvelous how Tolstoy can write from the perspective of a teenage girl, and her hopes and fears at her first ball are given just as much detail and significance as the scenes of the men going into battle.

Key Takeaways:

"'...And he's 'very nice, very, very nice. Only not quite my taste—he is so narrow, like the dining-room clock.... Don't you understand? Narrow, you know—gray, light gray...'

'What rubbish you're talking!' said the countess.

Natasha continued: 'Don't you really understand? Nicholas would understand... Bezukhov, now, is blue, dark-blue and red, and he is square.'" Natasha has a pattern of symbolism that no one in her family—except perhaps Nicholas—can understand. It is a counterpart to Pierre's interest in numerology; he, too, has few opportunities to share his mystical ideas with others.

"He reminded her of their first encounter in the Otradnoe avenue, and how she had been unable to sleep that moonlight night, and told her how he had involuntarily overheard her. Natasha blushed at that recollection and tried to excuse herself, as if there had been something to be ashamed of in what Prince Andrew had overheard." In true Tolstoy fashion, it seems at first that Natasha and Andrew are fated to be together—but things can and will change as time progresses.

Book 6: Chapters 18-24

What Happens?

The day after the ball, Andrew finds it difficult to work. His friends and colleagues, especially Speranski, suddenly seem unappealing to him. He doubts that any work they do will have any effect or significance, and his four busy months in Petersburg have been a waste.

Andrew visits the Rostovs the following day, and the count insists that he stay for dinner. After dinner, Natasha's singing brings tears to Andrew's eyes. He cannot sleep that night, and resolves to make more of his life while he still has vitality.

Berg and Vera throw a dinner party, which Pierre attends, along with both Andrew and Natasha. Both Pierre and Vera realize there is something developing between Andrew and Natasha. Vera indelicately cautions Andrew that Natasha may not be ready for marriage just yet, and mentions the childish attachment between her and Boris.

Andrew spends the following day at the Rostovs, and both he and Natasha realize their feelings for one another. Andrew's elderly father, however, insists that he wait a year before marrying her, so he proposes marriage on those terms. They quietly become engaged, and he goes abroad.

Analysis:

In writing these chapters about the love growing between Natasha and Andrew, Tolstoy never lets us forget about Pierre. The euphoric early feelings of love are constantly contrasted against Pierre's unhappiness with Helene, and the feelings he has for Natasha that he tries to stifle. Just as death is never far off from any of the characters, so unhappiness always seems to be lingering nearby, even at their happiest moments.

Andrew's love for Natasha also provides him with a better perspective on reality. He had been swept up in the busy activities of the charismatic politician, Speranski, but once his inner life revives through his love for the enchanting Natasha, he suddenly sees how false and manipulative the political players are. He realizes that his instinct to retire to private life, where his family is the priority, was the correct one after all.

Key Takeaways:

"'What does it matter to me or to Bitski what the Emperor was pleased to say at the Council? Can all that make me any happier or better?' And this simple reflection suddenly destroyed all the interest Prince Andrew had felt in the impending reforms." Andrew is an intellectual who reads a great deal, and has spent much time reflecting and agonizing over decisions and ideas. It is telling, then, that this simple, momentary thought changes the course of his life.

"'Why do I strive, why do I toil in this narrow, confined frame, when life, all life with all its joys, is open to me?' said he to himself. And for the first time for a very long while he began making happy plans for the future. He decided that he must attend to his son's education by finding a tutor and putting the boy in his charge, then he ought to retire from the service and go abroad, and see England, Switzerland and Italy. 'I must use my freedom while I feel so much strength and youth in me,' he said to himself. 'Pierre was right when he said one must believe in the possibility of happiness in order to be happy, and now I do believe in it. Let the dead bury their dead, but while one has life one must live and be happy!' thought he." Andrew is extremely hard-working, and the fact that he intends to work just as hard at his personal growth as he did his bureaucratic work suggests that he has not yet gained the necessary balance when it comes to life. Still, he has finally taken steps on the right path.

Book 6: Chapters 25-27

What Happens?

With Andrew gone to Switzerland, Mary cares for affairs at Bald Hills. The old prince is more irritable and unpleasant than ever, and cruelly attacks Mary's most sensitive concerns—her nephew and her religious faith. Mary still corresponds with Julie Karagina, whose brother has been killed in military service in Turkey. In her letter, she denies rumors that her brother is engaged to Natasha Rostova, and says she doubts he will ever re-marry.

Six months after his departure, Andrew writes to Mary from Switzerland that he is engaged to Natasha, and more resolved than ever to marry her. He explains that he did not tell Mary before because he did not want to make matters worse between father and daughter, but he now asks his sister to help convince their father to give his blessing, and to reduce the waiting period by four months. However, the always-domineering Prince Bolkonski seems to have become senile, and he declares that Andrew must wait until he is dead to marry, or else the old prince will marry Mademoiselle Bourienne to give Andrew a stepmother too. To Mary's horror, it seems that the old prince is spending more time with her companion, and may actually be trying to make his cruel joke a reality.

Desperate to escape the miserable household, Mary dreams of going on a religious pilgrimage. She even buys herself a peasant outfit to wear for her journey. Yet she cannot bear to be parted from her nephew and father. She is distressed to think that she loves her family more than God.

Analysis:

Andrew has already received his full inheritance from his father, and is far too old to require his consent to marry anyone. The fact that he so strongly desires his father to agree to his marriage reflects his personal honor code: he will not do anything against his father's wishes, if he can help it. Perhaps this is another form of the tyranny the old prince wields (like he does over Mary), just cloaked in the 19th century notions of gentlemanly honor.

Mary, meanwhile, has begun to realize—though not accept—that of her two devotions, faith and family, only the latter will give her fulfillment. Though she is already rather an "old maid" by the standards of her society, and though her arranged meeting with Anatole Kuragin (her only potential suitor) went so badly, deep down she still wants to be a wife and mother, not a religious pilgrim. She, too, has found the direction her life will take, though she has not yet reconciled herself to it.

Key Takeaways:

"The longer she lived, the more experience and observation she had of life, the greater was her wonder at the short-sightedness of men who seek enjoyment and happiness here on earth: toiling, suffering, struggling, and harming one another, to obtain that impossible, visionary, sinful happiness." The female lead characters in *War and Peace* seem to understand a little more than their male counterparts how important nourishing one's inner life is. Whether it is devotion to religious ideas, like Mary, or love of beauty and truth, like Natasha, the peaceful aspects of life must take precedence over war and struggle.

BOOK SEVEN

1810-1811

Book 7: Chapters 1-7

What Happens?

After several years with his regiment, Nicholas finally returns home to help his parents manage their financial difficulties. He becomes convinced that his father's manager, Mitenka, has embezzled funds, and loses his temper. Other than making a scene, Nicholas fails to do anything significant to help the family crisis and devotes his time to hunting instead.

One fine fall day, Natasha and Petya insist on joining Nicholas and his father on a wolf hunt. Natasha impresses everyone with her skill. Meanwhile, Count Rostov gets in the way and costs them several chances at catching the wolf, and finally goes home. The party later discovers a poacher, who turns out to be employed by Ilagin, a neighboring nobleman with whom the Rostovs have had difficulties. When confronted, Ilagin apologizes and invites everyone to hunt hares on his land. The hunters compete to see who has the fastest dog. A man whom the Rostov children call "Uncle" wins the competition.

The man invites the Rostovs to spend the night at his house. They agree, and have a wonderful time at the modest estate. They sing and dance to the balalaika with the servants. Despite never having seen or heard Russian peasant dances, Natasha becomes so enthralled in the music that she begins to dance in exactly the right style. Finally, their parents send a messenger to fetch them. On their way home, Nicholas and Natasha agree that this was one of the happiest and most peaceful nights of their lives.

Analysis:

These chapters contain one of the most famous scenes in *War and Peace*—the hunt, followed by Natasha's dance. The fact that Natasha instinctively knows how to do traditional Russian activities, despite being raised to imitate Western European high society, illustrates Tolstoy's belief in the notion that there are innate, inborn aspects of the Russian soul that no amount of French lessons and English dances can erase. Because the whole Rostov family yields to their feelings more easily than others, such as the repressed Bolkonski family, they are more in touch with their inner Russianness.

Key Takeaways:

"Once, when he had touched on this topic with his mother, he discovered, to his surprise and somewhat to his satisfaction, that in the depth of her soul she too had doubts about this marriage." Although Andrew is a good person, and a good match for Natasha, the Rostovs are uneasy about the marriage, partly because Natasha has a history of falling in and out of love easily, and partly because they realize how much Andrew's father objects to Natasha—and by extension, the whole family.

"'But you know, my dear boy, it's a pity you got excited! Mitenka has told me all about it.'

'I knew,' thought Nicholas, 'that I should never understand anything in this crazy world.'

'You were angry that he had not entered those 700 rubles. But they were carried forward—and you did not look at the other page.'

'Papa, he is a blackguard and a thief! I know he is! And what I have done, I have done; but, if you like, I won't speak to him again.'

'No, my dear boy' (the count, too, felt embarrassed. He knew he had mismanaged his wife's property and was to blame toward his children, but he did not know how to remedy it). 'No, I beg you to attend to the business. I am old. I...'

'No, Papa. Forgive me if I have caused you unpleasantness. I understand it all less than you do.'" This scene depicts in a nutshell the problem with the Russian aristocracy in the 19th century: according to the world's standards, they are educated, powerful people, and yet they have no ability even to understand the operations of

their estate, the source of their wealth, let alone manage it. They have no way of knowing whether their servant is cheating them—and no way to remedy it if he is.

"'No, I shan't have such luck,' thought Rostov, 'yet what wouldn't it be worth! It is not to be! Everywhere, at cards and in war, I am always unlucky.' Memories of Austerlitz and of Dolokhov flashed rapidly and clearly through his mind. 'Only once in my life to get an old wolf, I want only that!' thought he, straining eyes and ears and looking to the left and then to the right and listening to the slightest variation of note in the cries of the dogs." Nicholas, as we have seen before, is not as adept as Andrew and Pierre at expressing and analyzing his feelings, yet he feels deeply all the same. Capturing a wolf symbolizes for him his redemption as a competent human being, rather than the bumbling, hotheaded, immature boy he has been.

Book 7: Chapters 8-13

What Happens?

The Rostovs' financial crisis continues, even though they have continued to cut back on their expenses. They may have to sell their family home, Otradnoe. The countess feels that their only hope is to marry Nicholas to someone wealthy—and Julie Karagina seems to be the right choice. After some wavering, Nicholas decides to keep his word and marry Sonya, much to their disappointment. More than anything, though, the count and countess feel guilty and ashamed for mismanaging their money and putting Nicholas in such a position.

Meanwhile, Andrew writes to Natasha, saying that his health has forced him to stay abroad a bit longer. Natasha sinks into low spirits, though the family members all try to force themselves into a spirit of gaiety for the holidays. The children dress up and join in with mummers traveling around the neighborhood. Nicholas and Sonya find time to be alone and renew their relationship. Natasha almost immediately finds out that they again plan to marry.

Nicholas's parents are angry and accusative when they hear that Nicholas wants to marry Sonya. Since she is a poor relative, they blame her, not their own son, for the romance that has developed. Finally, they reach a truce wherein the countess will not be unkind to Sonya if Nicholas promises not to marry her in secret.

Analysis:

Natasha is convinced that Andrew's return is the only remedy for her restlessness and depression. It is not he himself she misses so—she barely knows him, really—but rather her own internal unease at the family's problems makes her pin all her hopes on her future marriage.

Nicholas, on the other hand, does not feel enough unease about the family problems—considering that his thoughtless gambling with Dolokhov greatly exacerbated the crisis. Yet he cannot bring himself to do the one thing that could remedy it: marry an heiress for her money. His affection for Sonya reawakens later; it seems to be primarily his own notions of honor that prevent him from even meeting with Julie Karagina.

Key Takeaways:

"'Sonya, is it well with thee?' he asked from time to time.

'Yes!' she replied. 'And with thee?'" After growing up together, when Nicholas came home from the front, he had forced Sonya to go back to their addressing each other formally. With their renewed romance, though, they are once again using the familiar pronoun.

"The countess, with a coldness her son had never seen in her before, replied that he was of age, that Prince Andrew was marrying without his father's consent, and he could do the same, but that she would never receive that intriguer as her daughter." The countess is aware that she is doing exactly the same thing as old Prince Bolkonski, yet she feels that she is in the right (just as strongly as the old Prince does).

BOOK EIGHT

1811-1812

Book 8: Chapters 1-5

What Happens?

Around the same time that Natasha and Andrew became engaged, Pierre's mentor, Joseph Bazdeev, died. Pierre is thus doubly gloomy, and has no one to keep his behavior in check anymore. He goes back to his old ways of heavy drinking and gambling in Moscow.

Old Prince Bolkonski and Mary move to Moscow. The prince still has political commitments, even though his dementia is starting to become apparent, and he treats Mary terribly as a result. She is also very lonely, missing her religious folk and finding no confidant in Moscow. It turns out that, in person, she and her pen pal Julie Karagina have little in common. The Bolkonskis host a name-day party on St. Nicholas's day, with a guest list dictated by the old prince. Boris Drubetskoy attends and shows interest in Mary, no doubt motivated by her fortune. Pierre was also in attendance and warns Mary that Boris is a fortune hunter who is trying to choose between her and Julie. Mary starts to confide in Pierre and begins to cry. To change the subject, she asks about Natasha, her future sister-in-law, whom she seems resolved to dislike.

In one of the most darkly comic chapters in the novel, Boris finally decides to propose to Julie. The fashion at the time is to act "melancholy" and talk about death, so Julie is convinced that she, as a wealthy and (in her own mind) attractive heiress, should adopt this attitude, and Boris follows suit. They drop the charade once they are officially engaged, and instead turn their minds to material concerns.

Analysis:

In settling for his old ways, Pierre realizes that he has sold out his ideals. He is deeply unhappy, as are Prince Nicholas Bolkonski and Mary. The old prince is angry that his life is at its end, that his once-powerful mind is now failing him, and that his children are determined to do the things of which he disapproves. After years of increasing cruelty at the hands of her father, Mary realizes that she is becoming domineering with her own nephew. The final specimen of misery is Boris, who is not a cruel or insensitive person, but who is constantly striving to climb socially to rescue himself and his mother from falling into poverty. He recognizes that Mary is a better person than Julie, but her father is in the way, so he chooses the easier path. He realizes, though, that he has "Renounced the possibility of true love."

Key Takeaways:

"He ceased keeping a diary, avoided the company of the Brothers, began going to the Club again, drank a great deal, and came once more in touch with the bachelor sets, leading such a life that the Countess Helene thought it necessary to speak severely to him about it. Pierre felt that she was right, and to avoid compromising her went away to Moscow." Pierre's diary, a symbol of his time spent as a spiritual seeker, has been abandoned: that chapter of his life is over. He then begins behaving so badly that his morally corrupt wife has to chastise him about it.

"How horrified he would have been seven years before, when he first arrived from abroad, had he been told that there was no need for him to seek or plan anything, that his rut had long been shaped, eternally predetermined, and that wriggle as he might, he would be what all in his position were. He could not have believed it! Had he not at one time longed with all his heart to establish a republic in Russia; then himself to be a Napoleon; then to be a philosopher; and then a strategist and the conqueror of Napoleon? Had he not seen the possibility of, and passionately desired, the regeneration of the sinful human race, and his own progress to the highest degree of perfection? Had he not established schools and hospitals and liberated his serfs? But instead of all that—here he was, the wealthy husband of an unfaithful wife, a retired gentleman-in-waiting, fond of eating and drinking and, as he unbuttoned his waistcoat, of abusing the government a bit, a member of the Moscow English Club, and a universal favorite in Moscow society. For a long time he could not reconcile himself to the idea that he was one of those same retired Moscow gentlemen-in-waiting he had so despised seven years before.

"Sometimes he consoled himself with the thought that he was only living this life temporarily; but then he was shocked by the thought of how many, like himself, had entered that life and that Club temporarily, with all their *teeth and hair, and had only left it when not a single tooth or hair remained."* This powerful passage summarizes Pierre's journey of the past seven years as one of heartbreaking futility. Yet he will take these experiences forward with him into the next chapters of his life.

"Sometimes he remembered how he had heard that soldiers in war when entrenched under the enemy's fire, if they have nothing to do, try hard to find some occupation the more easily to bear the danger. To Pierre all men seemed like those soldiers, seeking refuge from life: some in ambition, some in cards, some in framing laws, some in women, some in toys, some in horses, some in politics, some in sport, some in wine, and some in governmental affairs. 'Nothing is trivial, and nothing is important, it's all the same—only to save oneself from it as best one can,' thought Pierre. 'Only not to see it, that dreadful it!'" Pierre gives voice to what many of the characters are experiencing at this point in the novel—they are keeping busy with activities, but there are momentous changes and tests for them ahead.

"There was no need to say more: Julie's face shone with triumph and self-satisfaction; but she forced Boris to say all that is said on such occasions—that he loved her and had never loved any other woman more than her. She knew that for the Penza estates and Nizhegorod forests she could demand this, and she received what she demanded." In one last cynical twist, Tolstoy shows the true nature of marriages based on money.

Book 8: Chapters 6-11

What Happens?

Count Rostov must sell his estate, so the family goes to Moscow (minus the countess). They also prepare Natasha's trousseau for her wedding to Andrew. At the urging of her godmother, Marya Dmitrievna Akhrosimova, she and her father pay a visit to the Bolkonskis. The visit does not go well. The old prince refuses to see them, so the count leaves Natasha with Mary, who instantly dislikes her for her youthful and frivolous appearance. Mademoiselle Bourienne refuses to leave the room, so they carry on lengthy and forced chitchat, interrupted by the old prince, who wanders in wearing his dressing gown, having forgotten Natasha was there. Natasha coldly takes her leave. She is humiliated and in tears at home later that day.

The Rostovs go to the opera that evening. All of society seems to be present: Dolokhov is there in a Persian outfit, Boris and Julie sit and gossip, and Helene leads the pack of ladies wearing low-cut dresses. Helene's brother, Anatole, is there and takes notice of Natasha. Helene asks Natasha to sit with her for the third act. Anatole is wildly flirtatious (in early 19th century terms) and Natasha enjoys his attentions.

Anatole has been sent to Moscow by his father, who wants him to marry Julie or Mary to help settle his Petersburg debts. He cannot comply with his father's wishes, though, because he is already married. Two years earlier, in Poland, he had been forced to marry a girl he seduced. He paid off her father and abandoned her, but did not obtain a divorce.

Analysis:

Tolstoy sensitively and delicately depicted Natasha's scenes of finding her voice, attending her first ball, and discovering her native Russianness. She has been more in touch with nature and emotion than many of the other characters. Now, though, the author allows adult society to shatter her innocent world. She becomes aware of her own physical attractiveness and the sensual appeal of others, to the point that she cannot tell love from lust. Though her father and godmother try to protect her, unscrupulous people gain her trust and exploit it to their own selfish ends.

Key Takeaways:

Tolstoy uses the opera to symbolize Natasha's coming of age (and loss of innocence). To Natasha, the first act of the opera seems to her grotesque, unnatural, even nonsensical. Then she observes the people around her, especially the dazzling Helene Bezukhov whom she meets during the first intermission, and then the opera begins to make sense to her through its sensual stimulation. By the second act, she feels intoxicated by her surroundings, and the opera now seems natural and normal to her. In the third act, she has seemingly become a part of the staged drama, performing a role as she realizes she is the object of Anatole's interest and desire. She is unable to distinguish between truth and illusion.

Book 8: Chapters 12-22

What Happens?

Helene visits the Rostovs a few days after the opera, paying lots of insipid compliments. She invites them to a party, and they feel obligated to go. Count Rostov tries to guard his daughter and niece from the shady characters present at Helene's, but still Anatole manages to dance with Natasha and declare his love for her. That night, she decides she loves both Andrew and Anatole.

Marya Dmitrievna thinks the Rostovs should go back to Otradnoe to await Andrew's return, since the father is still so opposed to the wedding. Mary, meanwhile, has sent a letter of apology to Natasha, who does not know how to reply. She also receives a love letter from Anatole, in which he asks her to elope. She decides that she loves him, not Andrew. Sonya finds Anatole's letter, reads it, and is horrified. She confronts Natasha, who confirms that she wants Anatole now, but swears Sonya to secrecy. Natasha writes to Mary that she is breaking off the engagement with Andrew.

Meanwhile, Anatole and Dolokhov are planning the elopement. They obtain money, horses, and a defrocked priest to perform a fake wedding. But on the chosen night, Sonya and Marya Dmitrievna lock Natasha in her room, and send a servant to apprehend Anatole, but he escapes. Marya Dmitrievna is furious, but in order to prevent a duel, she promises not to tell Natasha's father about the attempted elopement. Natasha claims to be ill and keeps to her room. Anatole's brother-in-law, Pierre, is summoned to the house. Pierre informs them that Anatole is already married to a girl in Poland. Furious, Pierre finds Anatole and orders him to leave Moscow immediately. Anatole is indignant, but obeys. Natasha tries to poison herself, but immediately changes her mind and does not take the full dose. Still, she is very ill.

Pierre visits Andrew, who has finally returned to a changed Moscow. Andrew's one-time friend, Speranski, has been accused of deceit and forced into exile. Andrew wants Pierre to return Natasha's portrait to her and tell her that their relationship is over. Pierre complies, but finds that the distraught Natasha has understood everything already. Despite his compassion for her sadness, Pierre feels a new hopefulness growing in himself.

Analysis:

Natasha grew up with full confidence in her emotions and perceptions. As she follows her feelings, she hurts herself and those she cares about, and finally she realizes that she cannot trust her heart. Just as the opera was a false, distorted version of reality, so, too, are some feelings and even some people. When Andrew left for Europe, Natasha was forced to change her ideas about love: it is not just a joy, but also a test. Through loneliness, gullibility, and vanity, she fails that test. Andrew is not a man who can easily forgive failings in himself or others, and she feels the full effect of her transgression. Natasha is shattered, but she will overcome this lowest point in her life. She thus prefigures how Russia, devastated by its losses to the French, will summon its strength and drive out the invaders.

Key Takeaways:

"After reaching home Natasha did not sleep all night. She was tormented by the insoluble question whether she loved Anatole or Prince Andrew. She loved Prince Andrew—she remembered distinctly how deeply she loved him. But she also loved Anatole, of that there was no doubt. 'Else how could all this have happened?' thought she. 'If, after that, I could return his smile when saying good-by, if I was able to let it come to that, it means that I loved him from the first. It means that he is kind, noble, and splendid, and I could not help loving him. What am I to do if I love him and the other one too?' she asked herself, unable to find an answer to these terrible questions." Although her actions on the surface seem thoughtless, Natasha actually does agonize over her situation—she just does not have the strength or experience to make the right decision at this point in her life.

The end of this section includes one of the novel's most famous scenes, in which Pierre sees the Great Comet of 1811. This comet was a real astronomical occurrence; it was extremely bright and was visible for 260 days in 1811 and early 1812 (Comet Primer). When Tolstoy mentions that the comet portended the end of the world, he is referring to the popular belief that the comet was a bad omen. In retrospect, many people believed that the comet was a sign of Napoleon's invasion of Russia (Olson et al. 138). In *War and Peace*, it becomes a symbol of the happiness and inner peace that Pierre finds after dedicating himself to platonic and selfless love for Natasha. It further serves as something of a metaphor for Tolstoy's expansive ambition: he wishes to relate both the movements of the heavens and the inner workings of individuals, and in Pierre's reflections, we get one of many indications of how every element of life is in interplay with other elements.

BOOK NINE

1812

Book 9: Chapters 1-7

What Happens?

Starting Book Nine with a philosophical essay, Tolstoy contends that there is no rational explanation for the events of 1812—one would not expect so many coincidences and personality conflicts to amount to such a devastating war, but they did.

The French cross the Niemen River and march into Prussia, despite the fact that diplomatic negotiations are still going on. A number of Napoleon's men die in the process. Meanwhile, the Russian army had delayed at Vilna, faltering in choosing a defense strategy. Many members of the aristocracy join Alexander's court at Vilna, including Helene Bezukhova and Boris Drubetskoy. Boris eavesdrops on the Emperor and hears that Napoleon is invading.

Emperor Alexander sends an envoy, General Balashov, to Napoleon, who finally meets Napoleon with some difficulty. Balashov is so ineffectual that Napoleon seems to think he is an ally. He sends him off with a letter to Alexander that contains his refusal to withdraw. War has begun.

Analysis:

Prior to this book, the novel's sections were rather neatly divided by location and dramatis personae, and placed in logical (not always chronological) order. Now, though, the various timelines and characters are all converging in the chaos of the war.

In these chapters, Napoleon is depicted more critically than elsewhere in the novel. He is a comically self-important figure who is caught up in the ostentatious ceremony that surrounds him. This is not just humor at the expense of the so-called "great man," though: men die as a result of their sycophantic devotion to their Emperor. Alexander, too, appears to be a relatively weak leader; it seems that neither he nor Napoleon is fully in control of their military forces. The events that are taking place, then, are bigger than either man.

Key Takeaways:

"There are two sides to the life of every man, his individual life, which is the more free the more abstract its interests, and his elemental hive life in which he inevitably obeys laws laid down for him.

"Man lives consciously for himself, but is an unconscious instrument in the attainment of the historic, universal, aims of humanity. A deed done is irrevocable, and its result coinciding in time with the actions of millions of other men assumes an historic significance. The higher a man stands on the social ladder, the more people he is connected with and the more power he has over others, the more evident is the predestination and inevitability of his every action.

"The king's heart is in the hands of the Lord.

"A king is history's slave.

"History, that is, the unconscious, general, hive life of mankind, uses every moment of the life of kings as a tool for its own purposes." These meditations espouse some of Tolstoy's main ideas—and, indeed, reasons for writing *War and Peace.*

Book 9: Chapters 8-11

What Happens?

Prince Andrew wishes to duel with Anatole Kuragin, pursuing him first to Petersburg, then to Turkey, but never finding him. Andrew takes leave to Bald Hills, where he tries to address his increasingly tense family situation. He tries to confront his father about his poor treatment of Mary, and his inappropriate attachment to Mademoiselle Bourienne. The old prince, of course, does not listen to Andrew, and they do not reconcile before Andrew departs. Mary herself is full of forgiveness for her father.

Andrew returns to military headquarters, where he observes the many disagreeing groups as they argue about military strategy. He counts nine different schools of thought regarding the war. The ninth party, made up of many experienced statesmen, feel that the Emperor's presence itself is a hindrance and a danger to the war effort. Andrew shares this viewpoint, so he tactfully writes a letter to the Emperor suggesting that he needs to return to Moscow to drum up support for the war.

Alexander calls a meeting of men whose opinions he wishes to hear, and he invites Andrew. At this chaotic meeting, almost everyone is selfishly trying to distinguish himself, rather than offering the best advice for the war. The next day, Alexander offers Andrew a position in his own detachment, but Andrew declines it in favor of a job in the army.

Analysis:

When Andrew turns down an honored promotion and chance to belong to the Emperor's inner circle, he shows how much his values have changed. Only two years before, he was working to change military policy and reduce inefficiency. Now, by choosing to go to the front where he may be killed, he is demonstrating that what matters to him is to make meaning on the individual level, not to seek out glory in front of the whole army. Yet at the same time, the fact that he left without making peace with his father, and the fact that he should have realized that his interference would only make things worse for his sister, indicate that he has not yet fully learned to care for others as well as himself.

Key Takeaways:

"*After his betrothed had broken faith with him—which he felt the more acutely the more he tried to conceal its effects—the surroundings in which he had been happy became trying to him, and the freedom and independence he had once prized so highly were still more so. Not only could he no longer think the thoughts that had first come to him as he lay gazing at the sky on the field of Austerlitz and had later enlarged upon with Pierre, and which had filled his solitude at Bogucharovo and then in Switzerland and Rome, but he even dreaded to recall them and the bright and boundless horizons they had revealed.*" Natasha's betrayal seems to confirm the misanthropic ideas Andrew once had about the hollowness of life and love, and therefore all his earlier melancholy returns to him. He again devotes himself to the war effort, seemingly seeking out a way to die.

Book 9: Chapters 12-15

What Happens?

Nicholas Rostov has been with his hussar regiment at Vilna. He receives a letter from home, telling him the news of Natasha's illness and broken engagement. The family begs him to return home and help them again, but he makes no effort to ask for leave.

In a letter, Nicholas repeats his promise to Sonya that they will marry once he returns. He and all the other officers enjoy flirting with Mary Hendrikhovna, a German woman married to the regiment's doctor. He has taken on a protégé, a sixteen-year-old named Ilyin who looks up to him the way he once did to Denisov.

One night, the Pavlogradsky regiment is ordered to go to the village of Ostrovna. A battle begins and Nicholas fights bravely; however, when he commits violence in war, his conscience torments him. He wounds a French soldier, but cannot kill him; nevertheless, he earns the Cross of St. George.

Analysis:

In a similar manner to his sister, Natasha, Nicholas seems to abandon his fiancée for a fleeting attraction to a pretty stranger. All of the officers feel the same way about this woman, simply because they long for female companionship—not because of any real or lasting love. In this manner, Tolstoy shows that love is yet another ideal, like patriotism or religious faith, that is complicated and changeable as a person grows older and his or her circumstances change.

Key Takeaways:

"Since the campaigns of Austerlitz and of 1807 Rostov knew by experience that men always lie when describing military exploits, as he himself had done when recounting them; besides that, he had experience enough to know that nothing happens in war at all as we can imagine or relate it." Nicholas articulates the author's own views about the reason why history is not trustworthy. These are more than a little ironic in a work that sets out to tell a historical account.

"Formerly, when going into action, Rostov had felt afraid; now he had not the least feeling of fear. He was fearless, not because he had grown used to being under fire (one cannot grow used to danger), but because he had learned how to manage his thoughts when in danger. He had grown accustomed when going into action to think about anything but what would seem most likely to interest him—the impending danger. During the first period of his service, hard as he tried and much as he reproached himself with cowardice, he had not been able to do this, but with time it had come of itself." Having been a soldier himself, Tolstoy can offer the realistic perspective of how one feels during battle. With time, soldiers can train themselves mentally for combat, though they never fully get used to the danger.

Book 9: Chapters 16-23

What Happens?

Natasha is still so ill from her suicide attempt that her mother comes to Moscow, and the whole family tends to her while she recovers. Doctors give her all kinds of medicines and treatments, and the attention does more good for her than the supposed remedies. She tries to find solace in religion, attending church regularly and praying for others.

Pierre is in love with her, but he is also convinced that the world is ending. He feels called to play some important role that he has not yet discovered. Pierre is visiting the Rostovs when Sonya reads aloud a patriotic message from the government. Fifteen-year-old Petya Rostov distresses his parents by announcing that he wants to enlist. Meanwhile, suffering with unrequited love, Pierre decides it is too painful to visit the Rostovs, and resolves to stop.

The Emperor returns to Moscow. Petya sneaks out to attend the event, hoping to volunteer for the military directly to the tsar. Instead, he faints in the massive crowd. When he awakens, he is overcome with patriotic fervor. He threatens to run away from home if his parents do not allow him to enlist, so the count looks into getting the boy a safe assignment far from the front.

Pierre and Count Rostov attend a state dinner. Pierre makes an unpopular pronouncement that he believes the nobility should do more than just support the war effort materially; they should also advise the tsar. But then Alexander himself arrives and makes a powerful appeal for more support, and all in attendance resolve to give more.

Analysis:

Tolstoy delicately places the scene of Petya's adoration for the Emperor (with whom we just saw Andrew act in an utterly blasé manner) alongside the contagious patriotism at the state dinner, which gave Pierre such an immediate change of heart. All of these scenes help to explain why hundreds of thousands of men were willing to follow two fallible leaders even to their deaths. It is not that the individual emperors were so remarkable (as we have seen already, Napoleon has poor manners and Alexander is squeamish and a little gullible), but the emotion that the grandeur and ceremony inspired in the people was meaningful enough to motivate them.

The scenes between Pierre and Natasha show their respective growing maturity. Unlike Anatole, who felt no hesitation at the thought of seducing Natasha and ruining her reputation and prospects for marriage, Pierre knows he must love Natasha from afar.

Key Takeaways:

"It always seemed to her that everyone who looked at her was thinking only of what had happened to her. With a sinking heart, wretched as she always was now when she found herself in a crowd, Natasha in her lilac silk dress trimmed with black lace walked—as women can walk—with the more repose and stateliness the greater the pain and shame in her soul. She knew for certain that she was pretty, but this no longer gave her satisfaction as it used to. On the contrary it tormented her more than anything else of late." Gossip plays a powerful part in society, and so Natasha's torment continues because people continue to talk about her (or at least she believes they do).

BOOK TEN

1812

Book 10: Chapters 1-14

What Happens?

Napoleon's armies draw closer to Moscow. While Prince Bolkonski has been keeping busy quarreling with his children and making his will, the rest of the household realizes they may have to evacuate Bald Hills because the enemy troops are approaching. They send a messenger to Andrew, who is in Smolensk, to seek his advice, and he tells them to leave as soon as possible. Old Prince Nicholas refuses to believe the war is going that badly, and keeps busy at home.

In St. Petersburg, the two society matrons, Anna Pavlovna Scherer and Helene Bezukhova, continue to host their salons. News arrives that Kutuzov has been promoted to commander-in-chief of the military, and many at the salons disapprove, with the exception of Vasili Kuragin. Meanwhile, in another short episode, Captain Denisov's servant Lavrushka is captured by the French. He converses with Napoleon, who thinks he does not recognize him, and Lavrushka is able to convey some misleading information.

The Bolkonski household evacuates Bald Hills, stopping at Bogucharovo on their way to Moscow. Prince Bolkonski has a stroke. In one tender moment, he apologizes to Mary for treating her so badly, and then he has another stroke and dies. Mary soon finds herself in a dangerous situation—the peasants are planning to defect to the French. While they are searching for provisions to seize for their regiment, Nicholas Rostov and his protégé, Ilyin, find the peasants holding Mary captive and rescue her. Nicholas and Mary are drawn to one another, but he feels obligated to keep his promise to Sonya.

Analysis:

As the French invasion of Russia begins, the characters experience chaos in various ways. The old order collapses, symbolized by how the old aristocrat Nicholas Bolkonski dies and the peasants are rising up to seize power. Apart from this historical destiny, Tolstoy also looks to the destiny of individuals. Nicholas Rostov miraculously finds the woman who is fated to be his wife at the moment in which she needs help the most.

There is also a historical parallel in how Mary, as gentle and well-meaning as the Emperor Alexander, faces the rebellious peasants, whose fear of war has made them rise up in the same way that masses of people demanded Kutuzov as their leader.

Key Takeaways:

"'I write you in Russian, my good friend,' wrote Julie in her Frenchified Russian, 'because I have a detestation for all the French, and the same for their language which I cannot support to hear spoken... We in Moscow are elated by enthusiasm for our adored Emperor.'" Julie Drubetskaya writes to Mary in her poor Russian, because it is now unpatriotic to use French. Just as Julie had followed the trend of being melancholy earlier, she is now on the patriotism bandwagon, as are many others of the nobility. The nobility are still out of touch with reality, while the peasants are becoming desperate as they sense impending doom.

"The small, muddy, green pond had risen visibly more than a foot, flooding the dam, because it was full of the naked white bodies of soldiers with brick-red hands, necks, and faces, who were splashing about in it. All this naked white human flesh, laughing and shrieking, floundered about in that dirty pool like carp stuffed into a watering can, and the suggestion of merriment in that floundering mass rendered it specially pathetic." Prince Andrew sees the soldiers bathing in the pond at Bald Hills, and feels a premonition of the slaughter that will take place in battle once they continue on their way. His last visit to his ancestral estate is a melancholy one.

"'Dear one... Dearest...' Princess Mary could not quite make out what he had said, but from his look it was clear that he had uttered a tender caressing word such as he had never used to her before. 'Why didn't you come in?'

'And I was wishing for his death!' thought Princess Mary.

He was silent awhile.

'Thank you... daughter dear!... for all, for all... forgive!... thank you!... forgive!... thank you!...' and tears began to flow from his eyes. 'Call Andrew!' he said suddenly, and a childish, timid expression of doubt showed itself on his face as he spoke." On his deathbed, Prince Nicholas Bolkonski tries to make amends with Mary. When she tells him that Andrew is with the army at Smolensk, he says that Russia has perished and begins to weep.

"Ashamed as she was of acknowledging to herself that she had fallen in love with a man who would perhaps never love her, she comforted herself with the thought that no one would ever know it and that she would not be to blame if, without ever speaking of it to anyone, she continued to the end of her life to love the man with whom she had fallen in love for the first and last time in her life.

"Sometimes when she recalled his looks, his sympathy, and his words, happiness did not appear impossible to her. It was at those moments that Dunyasha noticed her smiling as she looked out of the carriage window.

"'Was it not fate that brought him to Bogucharovo, and at that very moment?' thought Princess Mary. 'And that caused his sister to refuse my brother?' And in all this Princess Mary saw the hand of Providence." Mary is completely different than Julie Karagina, who seemed to enjoy the fact that her wealth gave her power over her suitors (even if it was probably the main attraction that drew them). She resolves to keep her love secret in case it is not returned. Yet, she feels that the romance is destined, since Nicholas appeared at just the right moment to save her, and because Andrew and Natasha did not get married. Under Orthodox rules, two sets of siblings could not marry, because the family members became related at the first marriage.

Book 10: Chapters 15-25

What Happens?

Prince Andrew and Captain Denisov meet with General Kutuzov, who does not want to hear their ideas. He makes decisions on his own, based on experience and intuition. Kutuzov offers Andrew a job with him, but Andrew again declines a promotion in favor of staying with his army regiment.

The nobility are preparing to leave Moscow, but Julie Drubetskaya (formerly Karagina) holds one last soiree. She teases Pierre about his feelings for Natasha. The guests also gossip about Nicholas Rostov and Princess Mary. Pierre has overextended his (considerable) finances by volunteering his peasants for military service. He is depressed and longs to make some kind of real sacrifice.

Tolstoy interrupts the stories of his main characters and recounts what a disastrous battle Borodino was for both sides. He argues that both sides had poor strategies, made major mistakes, and should have avoided the battle.

Pierre is fleeing Moscow, but is moved by the sight of wounded soldiers and the expectation of twenty thousand more by the end of the battle. Then he sees a group of peasant soldiers in high spirits marching to war. He finds Boris Drubetskoy and asks to participate in the battle. He and Boris tour the encampment, and talk to both Kutuzov and Dolokhov. Count Bennigsen moves a regiment because he does not realize Kutuzov placed it there to ambush the French. Pierre is bored and does not understand what is going on. Later he visits Andrew, who expects to die the following day. Despite having intentionally put himself in this situation, Andrew is deeply unhappy and acts in a hostile manner toward Pierre, even though the latter brings the news that his remaining family is finally safe.

Analysis:

The Battle of Borodino was the turning point in the war, but the characters, of course, cannot know that in advance. Many characters see the need to make peace with themselves, their pasts, and their enemies, in case all is lost in the battle. Kutuzov kneels in prayer; Dolokhov and Pierre try to forget about the duel; and the characters who are not at the front seek to connect with one another. Mary and Nicholas, for the first time in many years, can each think of a possible future that would contain happiness and not struggle. Andrew, though, is not successful at reconciling with his past. He is still gathering observations and experience: he is fascinated by Kutuzov, who seems in touch with destiny and can understand his troops to their very souls.

Key Takeaways:

"Prince Andrew knew Denisov from what Natasha had told him of her first suitor. This memory carried him sadly and sweetly back to those painful feelings of which he had not thought lately, but which still found place in his soul. Of late he had received so many new and very serious impressions—such as the retreat from Smolensk, his visit to Bald Hills, and the recent news of his father's death—and had experienced so many emotions, that for a long time past those memories had not entered his mind, and now that they did, they did not act on him with nearly their former strength. For Denisov, too, the memories awakened by the name of Bolkonski belonged to a distant, romantic past, when after supper and after Natasha's singing he had proposed to a little girl of fifteen without realizing what he was doing. He smiled at the recollection of that time and of his love for Natasha, and passed at once to what now interested him passionately and exclusively." Andrew and Denisov meet, and find that the bond that connects them—Natasha—does not hold the same power over either one of them in the face of everything else going on.

"With the enemy's approach to Moscow, the Moscovites' view of their situation did not grow more serious but on the contrary became even more frivolous, as always happens with people who see a great danger approaching. At the approach of danger there are always two voices that speak with equal power in the human soul: one very reasonably tells a man to consider the nature of the danger and the means of escaping it; the other, still more reasonably, says that it is too depressing and painful to think of the danger, since it is not in man's power to fore-

see everything and avert the general course of events, and it is therefore better to disregard what is painful till it comes, and to think about what is pleasant. In solitude a man generally listens to the first voice, but in society to the second. So it was now with the inhabitants of Moscow." Perhaps no one but Kutuzov fully comprehends what is going to happen to Moscow.

"'But what is war? What is needed for success in warfare? What are the habits of the military? The aim of war is murder; the methods of war are spying, treachery, and their encouragement, the ruin of a country's inhabitants, robbing them or stealing to provision the army, and fraud and falsehood termed military craft. The habits of the military class are the absence of freedom, that is, discipline, idleness, ignorance, cruelty, debauchery, and drunkenness. And in spite of all this it is the highest class, respected by everyone. All the kings, except the Chinese, wear military uniforms, and he who kills most people receives the highest rewards.

'They meet, as we shall meet tomorrow, to murder one another; they kill and maim tens of thousands, and then have thanksgiving services for having killed so many people (they even exaggerate the number), and they announce a victory, supposing that the more people they have killed the greater their achievement. How does God above look at them and hear them?' exclaimed Prince Andrew in a shrill, piercing voice. 'Ah, my friend, it has of late become hard for me to live. I see that I have begun to understand too much. And it doesn't do for man to taste of the tree of knowledge of good and evil... Ah, well, it's not for long!' he added." Prince Andrew starts to express the author's own feelings regarding government, war, class, and human behavior. He shocks Pierre with the depths of his melancholy.

Book 10: Chapters 26-29

What Happens?

Stationed in the hills outside Moscow, Napoleon is preparing himself for war, mentally and physically. He receives an envoy from Paris, who brings a portrait of Napoleon's young son. Napoleon is aware that he must act the part of Emperor at all times, so he makes a show of contemplating the portrait then putting it away, because, he says, his son is too young to see battle.

On August 27, Napoleon inspects the locality, considers possible battle plans suggested by his men, and interacts with his generals. Napoleon unveils his battle plan. He shows polite interest in his men, and behaves in a much more mannerly way than he has been depicted in other parts of the book.

Tolstoy criticizes the battle plan Napoleon ultimately chose, because it was impractical. It took too long for word to get to him, so adjustments were never made in time. Tolstoy disagrees with historians who claim that Russia won the battle of Borodino simply because Napoleon had a cold. He repeats his frequent claim that history is predestined and one individual cannot change it, no matter how powerful that person is.

Analysis:

This section not only takes a detour into the enemy camp, but also, for the first time, the narration enters Napoleon's mind. We see him deliberating, choosing how to act. It is as if Tolstoy wants to remind us that he was just an ordinary person after all. The "great man" theory is just a myth—Napoleon is merely a person who acts a part well, and sometimes makes poor choices.

Key Takeaways:

"Though it was not clear what the artist meant to express by depicting the so-called King of Rome spiking the earth with a stick, the allegory apparently seemed to Napoleon, as it had done to all who had seen it in Paris, quite clear and very pleasing.

'The King of Rome!' he said, pointing to the portrait with a graceful gesture. 'Admirable!'

With the natural capacity of an Italian for changing the expression of his face at will, he drew nearer to the portrait and assumed a look of pensive tenderness. He felt that what he now said and did would be historical, and it seemed to him that it would now be best for him—whose grandeur enabled his son to play stick and ball with the terrestrial globe—to show, in contrast to that grandeur, the simplest paternal tenderness. His eyes grew dim, he moved forward, glanced round at a chair (which seemed to place itself under him), and sat down on it before the portrait. At a single gesture from him everyone went out on tiptoe, leaving the great man to himself and his emotion.

"So not one of the orders in the disposition was, or could be, executed. But in the disposition it is said that, after the fight has commenced in this manner, orders will be given in accordance with the enemy's movements, and so it might be supposed that all necessary arrangements would be made by Napoleon during the battle. But this was not and could not be done, for during the whole battle Napoleon was so far away that, as appeared later, he could not know the course of the battle and not one of his orders during the fight could be executed."

Book 10: Chapters 30-32

What Happens?

The battle is seen from Pierre's perspective. He registers the sensations of the battlefield, but cannot get caught up in the motivation for fighting. He follows a general to the battlefield without thinking what he is doing. The soldiers are annoyed with him at first for getting in the way, but soon find amusement at him. He is a sort of mascot for them.

Pierre unwittingly wanders to a hill that will become the central location of the battle. He is horrified when he sees mass slaughter. Mercifully, he is knocked unconscious by an explosion.

Later, when he recovers, he captures a French soldier accidentally. He lets him escape. The Russians rally and chase the French away from Pierre's area.

Analysis:

These are among the most graphic depictions of war violence in the entire book. Tolstoy's whole writing style seems to change to match the hectic fighting: his normally lengthy sentences become short, staccato, and gruesomely precise. What starts out as almost humorous—Pierre bumbling around in the way of the soldiers—becomes grotesque and tragic.

Key Takeaways:

"Pierre wished to be there with that smoke, those shining bayonets, that movement, and those sounds. He turned to look at Kutuzov and his suite, to compare his impressions with those of others. They were all looking at the field of battle as he was, and, as it seemed to him, with the same feelings. All their faces were now shining with that latent warmth of feeling Pierre had noticed the day before and had fully understood after his talk with Prince Andrew."

"One cannon ball, another, and a third flew over him, falling in front, beside, and behind him. Pierre ran down the slope. 'Where am I going?' he suddenly asked himself when he was already near the green ammunition wagons. He halted irresolutely, not knowing whether to return or go on. Suddenly a terrible concussion threw him backwards to the ground. At the same instant he was dazzled by a great flash of flame, and immediately a deafening roar, crackling, and whistling made his ears tingle.

When he came to himself he was sitting on the ground leaning on his hands; the ammunition wagons he had been approaching no longer existed, only charred green boards and rags littered the scorched grass, and a horse, dangling fragments of its shaft behind it, galloped past, while another horse lay, like Pierre, on the ground, uttering prolonged and piercing cries."

Book 10: Chapters 33-39

What Happens?

Tolstoy interrupts Pierre's battle story to describe the overall course of the combat. He blames the bloodshed on Napoleon's bad strategy and the chaos and disorganization of both sides.

Kutuzov and Napoleon cannot contain their emotion as both sides make mistakes and suffer huge losses. Napoleon is angry because the Russians are winning. Poor communication and insubordination have put the Russian troops in disarray, and this angers Kutuzov.

Both Anatole Kuragin and Andrew Bolkonski are wounded and presumed dead, but in actuality both are alive and in agony from their wounds. They are in the same hospital, and when Andrew sees how Anatole has lost his leg, he forgives Anatole for coming between him and Natasha.

Tens of thousands of men lie dead on the battlefield. When he realizes how many of his men have been killed, Napoleon is overcome with distress. Tolstoy editorializes that neither side really won; the losses were too great.

Analysis:

After Natasha's betrayal, Andrew first sought revenge against Anatole Kuragin. He chased him across several countries and back, and never found him. Failing to take his revenge, Andrew seemed intent on getting himself killed at the front. Several times, he refused promotions that would have taken him out of harm's way. It seemed that he was suicidal, but choosing a socially acceptable means of death. Yet when presented with the opportunity to step into the line of fire, he does not. He chooses to live, and in that moment is struck by a shot anyway. As an added irony, the man he had gone all the way to Turkey to try to kill is now dying in the same hospital with him. Andrew, though, has finally made peace with the past. After his sister's many pious speeches to him, he has finally embraced some small amount of spirituality.

Key Takeaways:

"'Can this be death?' thought Prince Andrew, looking with a quite new, envious glance at the grass, the wormwood, and the streamlet of smoke that curled up from the rotating black ball. 'I cannot, I do not wish to die. I love life—I love this grass, this earth, this air...' He thought this, and at the same time remembered that people were looking at him.

'It's shameful, sir!' he said to the adjutant. 'What...'

"He did not finish speaking. At one and the same moment came the sound of an explosion, a whistle of splinters as from a breaking window frame, a suffocating smell of powder, and Prince Andrew started to one side, raising his arm, and fell on his chest. Several officers ran up to him. From the right side of his abdomen, blood was welling out making a large stain on the grass." The thoughts that run through Andrew's mind as he spurns his earlier contemplation of suicide sound like things Natasha Rostova would have said to him years earlier. Life weighs too heavily on her now for her to feel simple enthusiasm for her surroundings, but after decades of misanthropy, Andrew finds those same feelings of delight.

"It was no longer a battle: it was a continuous slaughter which could be of no avail either to the French or the Russians." In this simple turn of phrase, Tolstoy perhaps sums up the entire section of the books, and perhaps even all of War and Peace: war is too costly to be worthwhile, in the author's opinion.

BOOK ELEVEN

1812

Book 11: Chapters 1-5

What Happens?

Tolstoy returns to one of his favorite topics: the limits of the historical process. He focuses on how Napoleon's actions were inevitable, just as Kutuzov's painful, unpopular decision to let the French occupy Moscow was.

The Russians are unable to attack the French a second time, so they retreat from Borodino. Kutuzov argues with his generals and decides to follow his own plan. The chief of staff, German-born Count Bennigsen, continues to try to gather power for himself—if Kutuzov's plan is successful, he will find a way to claim credit for himself, and if it fails, he will avoid blame. Kutuzov foresees the inevitability that Moscow will have to be abandoned.

The nobility evacuates the city. In the tsar's absence, Count Rostopchin is in charge of the city. He tries to discourage flight, to no avail. He calls the fleeing residents cowards, which they do not like, but they leave anyway. Muscovites do not want to submit even temporarily to French occupation.

Analysis:

These chapters deal with the acceptance of destiny. General Kutuzov could not have foreseen that the French would make it all the way to Moscow, but he recognizes that these events are in motion and cannot be stopped. They must play themselves out—and they do. Count Rostopchin, by contrast, does not accept that Moscow's fate cannot be changed. He ambitiously hopes that he can be the one who can change the course of events. He is wrong, of course, and his interference only makes the evacuation of Moscow more difficult and chaotic.

Key Takeaways:

"A modern branch of mathematics having achieved the art of dealing with the infinitely small can now yield solutions in other more complex problems of motion which used to appear insoluble.

"This modern branch of mathematics, unknown to the ancients, when dealing with problems of motion admits the conception of the infinitely small, and so conforms to the chief condition of motion (absolute continuity) and thereby corrects the inevitable error which the human mind cannot avoid when it deals with separate elements of motion instead of examining continuous motion.

"In seeking the laws of historical movement just the same thing happens. The movement of humanity, arising as it does from innumerable arbitrary human wills, is continuous." Tolstoy finds a new analogy for the force of history—mathematics. Instead of a "great man" directing events according to his will, history is made up of the tiny particles of individual free will. They add up to an overall course of events.

"For people accustomed to think that plans of campaign and battles are made by generals—as any one of us sitting over a map in his study may imagine how he would have arranged things in this or that battle—the questions present themselves: Why did Kutuzov during the retreat not do this or that? Why did he not take up a position before reaching Fili? Why did he not retire at once by the Kaluga road, abandoning Moscow? And so on. People accustomed to think in that way forget, or do not know, the inevitable conditions which always limit the activities of any commander in chief. The activity of a commander in chief does not all resemble the activity we imagine to ourselves when we sit at case in our studies examining some campaign on the map, with a certain number of troops on this and that side in a certain known locality, and begin our plans from some given moment. A commander in chief is never dealing with the beginning of any event—the position from which we always contemplate it. The commander in chief is always in the midst of a series of shifting events and so he never can at any moment consider the whole import of an event that is occurring. Moment by moment the event is imperceptibly shaping itself, and at every moment of this continuous, uninterrupted shaping of events the commander in chief is in the midst of a most complex play of intrigues, worries, contingencies, authorities, projects, counsels, threats, and deceptions and is continually obliged to reply to innumerable questions addressed to him, which constantly conflict with one another." Again, the author reminds us that Kutuzov should not be blamed for everything that happened, especially because he and other commanders could not have known what was going to happen until it was already underway. All commanders can do is react—and as a man of great experience and understanding, Kutuzov reacts better than most would in his position.

Book 11: Chapters 6-7

What Happens?

In Petersburg, Helene Bezukhova has two lovers who are on the verge of finding out about each other. Helene proposes marriage to each of them. Then she converts to Catholicism in an attempt to annul her marriage to Pierre.

The gossip about Helene and her two suitors spreads around the city, and almost no one in society questions the fact that she is already married. Marya Dmitrievna Akhrosimova confronts her publicly about it, but no one takes her seriously.

Helene's own mother has always been jealous of her. She now cautions her daughter that the Orthodox religion will not recognize the divorce, but Helene insists that the Pope himself will authorize it, so everyone else must accept it as fact. Helene decides to marry the elder of the two suitors. She tries to notify Pierre by letter.

Analysis:

Like her scheming father before her, Helene comes up with a plan so audacious it might work. Fortunately, she does not have any sentimental attachment to her first husband or her religious tradition, so she can exchange these for others without any qualms.

Her two suitors are also interesting: one is an older man, a grandee of the Russian Empire. The other, from whom Helene gets the idea to convert to Catholicism, is a young prince from another (unspecified) country. Helene uses the young prince for his connections, but ultimately chooses the older man. Helene's friend, the diplomat, Bilibin, says that she should marry the Russian man to secure her position in society, then when he dies she can marry the prince. He may be joking, but it seems to be the plan that Helene adopts.

Key Takeaways:

"And as it always happens in contests of cunning that a stupid person gets the better of cleverer ones, Helene— having realized that the main object of all these words and all this trouble was, after converting her to Catholicism, to obtain money from her for Jesuit institutions (as to which she received indications)—before parting with her money insisted that the various operations necessary to free her from her husband should be performed. In her view the aim of every religion was merely to preserve certain proprieties while affording satisfaction to human desires." In this remarkably cynical digression from the battlefield to Petersburg, Tolstoy can get away with a cutting critique of organized religion because it is Catholicism, which Russian Orthodoxy considers "false religion" and vice versa. While Pierre's Freemason acquaintances were depicted as apathetic and disorganized, the Catholic men who help Helene convert are shown to be money-grubbing, lustful towards Helene, and easily outwitted by her.

"By the beginning of August Helene's affairs were clearly defined and she wrote a letter to her husband—who, as she imagined, loved her very much—informing him of her intention to marry N.N. and of her having embraced the one true faith, and asking him to carry out all the formalities necessary for a divorce, which would be explained to him by the bearer of the letter.

"'And so I pray God to have you, my friend, in His holy and powerful keeping—Your friend Helene.'

"This letter was brought to Pierre's house when he was on the field of Borodino." The fact that Helene imagines Pierre to "love her very much" shows the depth of her narcissism (and that, social scheming aside, she really is not very clever). The timing of the letter, sent by a spoiled, shallow wrongdoer to a man witnessing the atrocities of war, is particularly compelling.

Book 11: Chapters 8-11

What Happens?

Pierre is following the retreating army. He enjoys a simple meal with some soldiers, posing as a man of lesser means while with them. He wishes he had been born into more humble circumstances.

He sleeps in a carriage, and has an epiphany of sorts as he begins to process what he has just experienced. The next morning, he learns that Anatole Kuragin and Andrew Bolkonski have died.

When he arrives in Moscow, he is immediately summoned to Count Rostopchin. While waiting to meet with him, Pierre hears rumors about the surrender of the city—and that there is trouble with his wife. The count questions him about several Freemasons who have been arrested on charges of treason. Count Rostopchin advises him to flee Moscow before the French arrive. When he goes home, he finds his wife's letter. So much bad news is too much for him, so he sneaks away early the next morning.

Analysis:

Pierre realizes that he has missed out on having a communal life, like peasants and soldiers do. Like Natasha, deep in his soul he has an affinity for the ancient Russian ways, despite all of his Europeanized education. When he returns to his home, people immediately try to resume business dealings with him, but he is tired of these relationships based on his wealth and connections. Pierre runs away, rather than fall into the old patterns of his life. Just as Kutuzov, the hero of Russia, accepted destiny as it came (not how he would have wanted it to be), so Pierre, too, the hero of *War and Peace*, must accept the good and bad news and embrace his own destiny.

Key Takeaways:

"'To endure war is the most difficult subordination of man's freedom to the law of God,' the voice had said. 'Simplicity is submission to the will of God; you cannot escape from Him. And they are simple. They do not talk, but act. The spoken word is silver but the unspoken is golden. Man can be master of nothing while he fears death, but he who does not fear it possesses all. If there were no suffering, man would not know his limitations, would not know himself. The hardest thing [Pierre went on thinking, or hearing, in his dream] is to be able in your soul to unite the meaning of all. To unite all?' he asked himself. 'No, not to unite. Thoughts cannot be united, but to harness all these thoughts together is what we need! Yes, one must harness them, must harness them!' he repeated to himself with inward rapture, feeling that these words and they alone expressed what he wanted to say and solved the question that tormented him." Half dreaming, Pierre formulates the philosophy to which he will adhere in the future. He had been longing to hear Joseph Bazdeev's voice telling him what to do, but this new outlook on life comes from within himself. It incorporates what he learned from Bazdeev, but from now on he will not need anyone to tell him what to do.

Book 11: Chapters 12-17

What Happens?

The Rostovs, in typical fashion, have procrastinated, despite all of the news and reports indicating that they should leave Moscow. The countess is worried about Petya, who is enjoying army service and not thinking of danger. She arranges for him to transfer to a regiment that Pierre is organizing, which will be far from the front lines. Petya comes home on leave just as the French are on the brink of invading the city.

Natasha volunteers the Rostov house to the war effort, to use as an infirmary, and the family packs up their possessions. One of the wounded soldiers brought into the house is Andrew Bolkonski, but everyone feels it is best to conceal this from Natasha. Count Rostov allows the family's carts to be used to transport the wounded, not fully realizing this means they will lose all their possessions. The countess does, and throws a tantrum. Vera's husband, Berg, shows up to borrow some money, because he is shopping the possessions people are selling as they leave.

As they ride out of the city, Natasha notices Pierre walking on the street, dressed as a peasant. They stop him to talk, and he says he is going to stay in Moscow and fight. He seems distracted and nervous, but the Rostovs do not notice, and they continue on their way.

Analysis:

Napoleon had thought that Russians would stay and be conquered rather than lose their material things. He was wrong. Rich and poor alike value their freedom too much, and they flee. As the archetype of the generous Russian soul, the Rostovs first offer their once-splendid home to the wounded soldiers. Then they spend days packing their belongings, only to realize that their duty to their fellow human beings is to take the soldiers with them out of Moscow. Natasha and her father make these decisions to help others in an instant, because they know it is the right thing to do. Even the countess eventually realizes that they must keep their family safe and help others.

Key Takeaways:

"Natasha was gay because she had been sad too long and now nothing reminded her of the cause of her sadness, and because she was feeling well. She was also happy because she had someone to adore her: the adoration of others was a lubricant the wheels of her machine needed to make them run freely—and Petya adored her. Above all, they were gay because there was a war near Moscow, there would be fighting at the town gates, arms were being given out, everybody was escaping—going away somewhere, and in general something extraordinary was happening, and that is always exciting, especially to the young." While Sonya helps the family get ready to pack up and leave, Petya and Natasha are no help at all; they are having fun together. Petya is happily looking forward to the battles that are sure to take place soon, and Natasha can finally forget her sadness over Andrew and live in the moment as she once did. This moment of happiness will be fleeting for both of them.

Book 11: Chapters 18-25

What Happens?

Pierre has been living at the home of his old mentor, Joseph Bazdeev. Ostensibly this was to save some of his late mentor's books, but Pierre's mental state is worsening, and a terrible plan is starting to take shape. He asks a servant for some peasant clothes to wear—and a pistol.

Napoleon prepares to take over Moscow, which he does not know is nearly empty. He imagines that his government will teach the backward Russians how to live in a civilized manner. He plans to make a grand entrance into the city, and his men do not have the courage to tell him the true state of the city.

Russian troops try to evacuate wounded soldiers out of the city, but a panicked crowd of civilians is blocking the bridge. The army has to pretend it will open fire on the crowd to get them to move. Some of the soldiers, blocked from leaving the city, start looting instead.

The aristocrats, merchants, and police are gone, so there is disorder and violence among those who remain in Moscow. Rostopchin is irritated at being slighted by Kutuzov, and he is hopelessly unprepared for the position in which he finds himself. He orders that the lunatics should be let out of the asylum into the town. He lies to the angry mob that comes to his door, stalling so he that can get his carriage ready to leave. He offers one of the Freemason prisoners, Vereshchagin, to the crowd, telling them that the latter is a traitor. They lynch him. Rostopchin flees the city, and on his way out he meets a madman who has delusions of being Christ. The count encounters Kutuzov, and tries to blame him for the terrible state of the city.

Analysis:

Like Helene Bezukhova, Count Rostopchin is incredibly selfish and morally bankrupt. Unlike Kutuzov, he fights against the inevitable, the destiny of the city. He cannot succeed, of course, and in the process, he harms others. The bizarre scene in which he offers up an innocent criminal to the crowd is reminiscent of the New Testament story of Pilate offering up Christ and Barabbas to the Jews. The religious scenery continues as a madman (one of the asylum inmates who was freed on Rostopchin's order) raves in words reminiscent of Christ.

Key Takeaways:

"The view of the strange city with its peculiar architecture, such as he had never seen before, filled Napoleon with the rather envious and uneasy curiosity men feel when they see an alien form of life that has no knowledge of them. This city was evidently living with the full force of its own life. By the indefinite signs which, even at a distance, distinguish a living body from a dead one, Napoleon from the Poklonny Hill perceived the throb of life in the town and felt, as it were, the breathing of that great and beautiful body.

"Every Russian looking at Moscow feels her to be a mother; every foreigner who sees her, even if ignorant of her significance as the mother city, must feel her feminine character, and Napoleon felt it.

'Cette ville asiatique aux innombrables eglises, Moscou la sainte. La voila done enfin, cette fameuse ville! Il etait temps,'* said he, and dismounting he ordered a plan of Moscow to be spread out before him, and summoned Lelorgne d'Ideville, the interpreter.

* 'That Asiatic city of the innumerable churches, holy Moscow! Here it is then at last, that famous city. It was high time.'"

Moscow is Russia's "Ancient and sacred capital" and even Napoleon is impressed by it. He calls it an "Asiatic" city, agreeing with those in the late 19th century who claimed that Russia's true ties were with the East, not the West.

"In a queenless hive no life is left though to a superficial glance it seems as much alive as other hives." Tolstoy uses a Homeric simile comparing the deserted city of Moscow to a bee hive without a queen. There is some small activity going on that fools Napoleon at first into thinking the people have stayed.

Book 11: Chapters 26-29

What Happens?

The French forces enter the city and begin looting. Much of the city has been set on fire, and over the next few days it burns to the ground. Each side blames the other for setting the fires, but, ever the contrarian, Tolstoy argues that it was accidental.

Pierre is devastated from the trauma of war, the death of his best friend, the persecution of Freemasons, and the end of his marriage. His mental breakdown takes the form of a plan to assassinate Napoleon. After killing the Emperor, he would certainly be caught and killed. He wants to be a martyr, but a heroic one.

At Bazdeev's house, however, a French captain spares the life of Bazdeev's mentally disabled brother, and makes friends with Pierre. The two end up enjoying a pleasant dinner. Pierre feels guilty for liking Captain Ramballe, but he does. He even confides to him about his love for Natasha.

Analysis:

In his plan to kill Napoleon, Pierre of course seeks to commit a violent act, but his motive is to help humanity. The more he sees violent acts, the more he comes back to himself. He cannot allow a French officer to be shot (with the very gun he plans to use on Napoleon). The officer assumes Pierre must be French, even though he has been trying to conceal it. He is wrong—Pierre has finally started to comprehend the nature of belonging to humanity without national borders.

Key Takeaways:

"In reality, however, it was not, and could not be, possible to explain the burning of Moscow by making any individual, or any group of people, responsible for it. Moscow was burned because it found itself in a position in which any town built of wood was bound to burn, quite apart from whether it had, or had not, a hundred and thirty inferior fire engines. Deserted Moscow had to burn as inevitably as a heap of shavings has to burn on which sparks continually fall for several days. A town built of wood, where scarcely a day passes without conflagrations when the house owners are in residence and a police force is present, cannot help burning when its inhabitants have left it and it is occupied by soldiers who smoke pipes, make campfires of the Senate chairs in the Senate Square, and cook themselves meals twice a day." Tolstoy insists that all the fires were accidental and that the French had no reason to burn anything.

"He began to explain that he understood love for a woman somewhat differently. He said that in all his life he had loved and still loved only one woman, and that she could never be his.

"'Tiens!' said the captain.

"Pierre then explained that he had loved this woman from his earliest years, but that he had not dared to think of her because she was too young, and because he had been an illegitimate son without a name. Afterwards when he had received a name and wealth he dared not think of her because he loved her too well, placing her far above everything in the world, and especially therefore above himself." Pierre's disclosure that he has always loved Natasha may be the first time he has ever admitted such a fact out loud to himself or others. That he never thought he was worthy of her offers a new explanation of why he felt such guilt every time he engaged in some kind of bad conduct.

Book 11: Chapters 30-32

What Happens?

With the road so crowded with fleeing Muscovites, the Rostovs do not cover much distance. The first night, from their vantage point 14 miles away, they watch their city burn. The conditions are perfect for the fire to spread, and it does. The servants weep for the city.

Natasha finds out that Andrew is with them, and is in shock for a long time. Finally, she goes to see him, uncertain of what condition she will find him in, and even more uncertain at how he will receive her. He forgives her wordlessly, holding out his hand.

Andrew is in severe pain and often hallucinates, so he is not sure at first whether Natasha is real or another hallucination—he is trying to summon the feeling of universal love he felt in the hospital. Natasha is real, but she helps him regain some of that feeling anyway. She tends to him day and night from then on.

Analysis:

Andrew has found a new sense of spiritual purpose and has renewed his capacity for forgiveness and compassion. This empowers him to try to recover, and he has made some progress. His injuries, though, are grave. Even this reconciliation with Natasha seems to sadden those around him. They cannot speak of the possibility of a renewed engagement—it seems unlikely that he will live very much longer.

Key Takeaways:

"'Who's to put it out?' Daniel Terentich, who had hitherto been silent, was heard to say. His voice was calm and deliberate. 'Moscow it is, brothers,' said he. 'Mother Moscow, the white...' his voice faltered, and he gave way to an old man's sob.

"And it was as if they had all only waited for this to realize the significance for them of the glow they were watching. Sighs were heard, words of prayer, and the sobbing of the count's old valet." Many had felt that the exodus from Moscow would only be a temporary one. With the burning of the buildings, it was clear that they could never return to the city they had left, even if they went back to the geographic location.

"'Forgive me!' she whispered, raising her head and glancing at him. 'Forgive me!'

'I love you,' said Prince Andrew.

'Forgive...!

'Forgive what?' he asked.

'Forgive me for what I ha-ve do-ne!' faltered Natasha in a scarcely audible, broken whisper, and began kissing his hand more rapidly, just touching it with her lips.

'I love you more, better than before,' said Prince Andrew, lifting her face with his hand so as to look into her eyes." Andrew has been entirely changed by his experiences. He is no longer the proud man who cannot stand insults to his honor, no longer the cynical man who could not believe in pure love. He forgives Natasha, and she, too, can finally be at peace.

Book 11: Chapters 33-34

What Happens?

Pierre is forced to put aside his plan to kill Napoleon, and instead come to the aid of those still living in the city under French occupation. First, as a house burns, a mother is distressed because her little daughter is, she thinks, still inside. Pierre and a servant go looking for the child, and some French soldiers pause from their looting to direct them to the child hiding in the garden.

The child is unwilling to go with Pierre, so he carries her, struggling, back to where the family had been. They are no longer there. Pierre cannot find the girl's family, so he gives the child to a woman who claims to know the mother.

Pierre sees a pair of French soldiers robbing an Armenian man and evidently planning to rape the daughter of the man. He attacks one of the soldiers. Some French officers see the assault and arrest Pierre.

Analysis:

Pierre's "madness," his impractical plan of killing Napoleon, is discarded as real problems present themselves. For the first time in several days, he has to think in practical terms instead of the numerology and mysticism into which he had retreated. He has found a way to serve others more meaningfully than assassinating Napoleon.

The French soldiers have lost the veneer of military training. They are confused looters trying to find food and supplies in an unfamiliar city. They are a particular threat to the women still remaining in Moscow. But their treatment of Pierre shows that they are also more patient than they would have been with him on the battlefield.

Key Takeaways:

"'There's a child in that house. Haven't you seen a child?' cried Pierre.

'What's he talking about? Get along!' said several voices, and one of the soldiers, evidently afraid that Pierre might want to take from them some of the plate and bronzes that were in the drawer, moved threateningly toward him.

'A child?' shouted a Frenchman from above. 'I did hear something squealing in the garden. Perhaps it's his brat that the fellow is looking for. After all, one must be human, you know...'" It seems Pierre would have even gone into the burning building looking for the child, had the soldiers not helpfully pointed him in the right direction (while they helped themselves to the possessions left behind in Moscow).

BOOK TWELVE

1812

Book 12: Chapters 1-3

What Happens?

Meanwhile in Petersburg, society still meets at Anna Pavlovna's to gossip. The topic *du jour* is Helene Bezukhova, who has fallen ill. The rumor has it that it is a heart problem, Helene will not permit anyone to visit, and she is using an Italian doctor instead of any Russian ones. Anna Pavlovna predicts that the next day, they will receive news.

Her presentiment is correct: the city receives positive news from Kutuzov, and they assume there was a victory. They rejoice, until more news arrives later: Helene has died. Officially, the cause is said to be angina pectoris, but the rumor spreads that the Italian doctor was giving her an abortion drug and she overdosed. The death is thought to be a suicide because Pierre did not respond to the letter asking for a divorce.

Then Emperor Alexander receives the word that Moscow has been lost, and several persons who were court favorites have been killed. Rostopchin wastes no time in trying to sow seeds of displeasure regarding Kutuzov's performance. Just as society needs to blame someone for Helene's death—they have an old habit of always blaming Pierre for Helene's self-inflicted problems—so they are quick to blame Kutuzov for the whole disastrous battle of Borodino, even though he was one of three commanders.

Analysis:

Gossip has been a key device in the telling of the stories of *War and Peace*—the characters find out many things about one another, some of which are true, and even the false gossip affects their lives and reputations. Helene has lived entirely in the little aristocratic world of Petersburg drawing rooms, so instead of any deathbed scenes, the only reports we receive of her illness and death are through hearsay. Just as the reader never learned whether Pierre's suspicions of Dolokhov's affair with Helene were truly justified, the circumstances of Helene's death are never revealed either—it may have been an accident, or suicide, or truly a heart illness.

Key Takeaways:

"Kutuzov wrote that the Russians had not retreated a step, that the French losses were much heavier than ours, and that he was writing in haste from the field of battle before collecting full information. It followed that there must have been a victory. And at once, without leaving the church, thanks were rendered to the Creator for His help and for the victory." Though later the people are angry with Kutuzov, he never actively tried to mislead them; they jumped to conclusions prematurely.

"'Well, then, go back to the army,' he said, drawing himself up to his full height and addressing Michaud with a gracious and majestic gesture, 'and tell our brave men and all my good subjects wherever you go that when I have not a soldier left I shall put myself at the head of my beloved nobility and my good peasants and so use the last resources of my empire. It still offers me more than my enemies suppose,' said the Emperor growing more and more animated; 'but should it ever be ordained by Divine Providence,' he continued, raising to heaven his fine eyes shining with emotion, 'that my dynasty should cease to reign on the throne of my ancestors, then after exhausting all the means at my command, I shall let my beard grow to here' (he pointed halfway down his chest) 'and go and eat potatoes with the meanest of my peasants, rather than sign the disgrace of my country and of my beloved people whose sacrifices I know how to appreciate.'" The Emperor Alexander makes an inspiring speech about not giving up the fight. Interestingly, though, it contains a hint of later history. When Alexander died in 1825 (at a time when his popularity was at a nadir), rumors circulated that the closed casket at his funeral was actually empty, and that not long afterwards, a mysterious religious hermit appeared in Siberia, whose grave the royal family would visit in future years. So contemporary audiences would have been captivated by this scene in which Alexander speaks of adopting the life of a peasant.

Book 12: Chapters 4-8

What Happens?

Nicholas is sent to the city of Voronezh to buy horses for the army, and is enjoying the attention he receives as a visitor. He attends a soiree thrown by at a local governor's home. Flirting shamelessly with an official's wife, he makes a bit of a spectacle of himself and annoys the husband.

The story of his rescue of Mary Bolkonskaya has reached the guests, including Mary's aunt, whom he meets at the party. The hostess wants to help arrange a marriage, and Nicholas seems to reluctantly agree that she can test the waters for him. Mary is still in mourning for her father, so everything must be done discreetly.

Nicholas visits Mary, who comes to stay with her family in the same province. He is drawn to her, despite his pangs of conscience regarding Sonya. Reflecting the love she feels within, Mary's face becomes more beautiful and she has a confidence that she has never had before—even Mademoiselle Bourienne is impressed. Nicholas finds a new optimism for life that he has not felt in a long time.

Nicholas goes to church (where Mary is, of course) and prays for release from his obligation to Sonya. A letter arrives from Sonya, ending their engagement. The countess herself sends a letter informing Nicholas that the Rostovs have Andrew with them in Yaroslavl. When Mary hears the news, she immediately sets off to see him.

It turns out that Countess Rostova forced Sonya to send the letter. As a poor relation living with the family, Sonya knows she is indebted to the Rostovs and cannot refuse what they ask of her. She hopes that her letter will have the opposite effect and strengthen his resolve to marry her. Failing that, she also has the hope that Andrew might recover and marry Natasha, in which case another marriage would not be possible between the two families.

Analysis:

The Rostovs need Nicholas to marry someone wealthy, and though that idea is distasteful to him, it seems that Mary could make both Nicholas and his parents happy. The love triangle is a poignant one, though, because both Mary and Sonya have led stifled, self-sacrificing lives, and one of them must continue to sacrifice her feelings for the good of her family.

Key Takeaways:

"In the highest spirits Nicholas arrived at night at a hotel in Voronezh, ordered things he had long been deprived of in camp, and next day, very clean-shaven and in a full-dress uniform he had not worn for a long time, went to present himself to the authorities." Tolstoy begins the chapter with remarks on how ordinary life went on for most people, and how those most involved with the events of history are often the ones who think about it the least. Nicholas did not feel it was his duty to worry about the big questions of the war; he would have said that was Kutuzov's job. So he is happy to get away from his regiment, even at this critical moment in history, and enjoy some little luxuries he has missed.

Book 12: Chapters 9-13

What Happens?

Pierre is held prisoner by the French. He is held with the common criminals, the dregs of society, who can tell that he is upper class and therefore dislike him. He is interrogated for show, but it is clear that his answers do not matter and he will be found guilty of a crime—evidently, it will be arson, because he was near a fire.

In a second interrogation, the officer acts willing to believe Pierre's story of saving Captain Ramballe's life, but then Pierre seems to be included with the group of prisoners to be executed. It turns out, though, that these prisoners were supposed to watch as other prisoners are executed, as a warning. The soldiers who commit the executions are shaking and clearly do not want to participate. They try to hide the bodies as quickly as possible.

Pierre is taken to a ruined church, where he is held with twenty other prisoners. Sitting in shock from the trauma of what he has just witnessed, Pierre unconsciously watches one of the other men. The man starts talking to him, and gives him a baked potato to eat. His name is Platon Karataev and he and the other men are from a captured regiment. He speaks with many proverbs, but can never repeat himself.

Pierre is held prisoner for four weeks. He admires Platon for his kindness, energy, and many skills. They have long talks, and Pierre's spirit begins to heal from its wounds.

Analysis:

Although Tolstoy does not usually use symbolic names for his characters, the name Platon is at least telling, if not wholly symbolic. Platon is the Russian version of the Greek name Plato, the name of the ancient philosopher. Typically, the Russian nobility always used the names of famous Christian saints (e.g., Nicholas, Alexander, Andrew, Peter), while peasants used names of "pagan" Greco-Roman origin such as Platon. So Karataev's name marks him as a peasant. Of course, someone who loves to talk in pithy sayings does seem to be a kind of philosopher, so his being the namesake of Plato seems appropriate. Lastly, it is in Plato's honor that the ideal of non-romantic love between friends—*platonic love*—is named, and certainly Pierre feels a friendly affection for his latest mentor. Platon will shape Pierre's ideals for the rest of his life.

Key Takeaways:

"From the moment Pierre had witnessed those terrible murders committed by men who did not wish to commit them, it was as if the mainspring of his life, on which everything depended and which made everything appear alive, had suddenly been wrenched out and everything had collapsed into a heap of meaningless rubbish. Though he did not acknowledge it to himself, his faith in the right ordering of the universe, in humanity, in his own soul, and in God, had been destroyed. He had experienced this before, but never so strongly as now. When similar doubts had assailed him before, they had been the result of his own wrongdoing, and at the bottom of his heart he had felt that relief from his despair and from those doubts was to be found within himself. But now he felt that the universe had crumbled before his eyes and only meaningless ruins remained, and this not by any fault of his own. He felt that it was not in his power to regain faith in the meaning of life." Before the arrest, Pierre had been making great strides on his spiritual journey. Now, however, his terrible experiences have dashed the beautiful thoughts and dreams that had been growing within him. He is starting over again, building up his inner self from a blank slate to a complex, caring man.

"To all the other prisoners Platon Karataev seemed a most ordinary soldier. They called him "little falcon" or "Platosha," chaffed him good-naturedly, and sent him on errands. But to Pierre he always remained what he had seemed that first night: an unfathomable, rounded, eternal personification of the spirit of simplicity and truth. Platon Karataev knew nothing by heart except his prayers. When he began to speak he seemed not to know how he would conclude." Pierre's first impression of Platon—his being round—endures, and is symbolic of how well-rounded a person he is. Unlike anyone else who has influenced Pierre—from the vain, insincere Emperor Napoleon to the mystic Joseph Bazdeev—Platon is a balanced person, not a single-minded fanatic.

Book 12: Chapters 14-16

What Happens?

Princess Mary takes her nephew and Mlle. Bourienne and goes to visit her brother, who is still in the care of the Rostovs. When she arrives, Mary cannot get information about Andrew out of anyone, and is nearly ready to cry in frustration. Finally, Natasha sadly informs her that his condition suddenly worsened two days ago.

Andrew is disconnecting from life. He tries to appear excited to see his son, and interested in the burning of Moscow, but he is weary. In a detached manner, he advises Mary to marry Nicholas. He cannot bring himself to tell her of the spiritual things he now believes. She prays for his soul.

The reason for the change in him is that two days before, he had a dream in which he died, and it made him see the need to stop fighting to live when he is so far gone. Before the dream, he had told Natasha how much he loves her, and fell asleep. Their love was the last connection to life that made him want to live, and the desire for death finally wins out over it. This starts the process of his life force slipping away.

He slips into unconsciousness, and still Natasha and Mary keep a vigil over his body until finally he expires. Everyone weeps for him.

Analysis:

The scene of Andrew's death is similar to another one of Tolstoy's later stories, *The Death of Ivan Ilyich*, in which a dying man has a deeply spiritual experience while everyone around him thinks of mundane or petty concerns. In the same way, Andrew's experience of death is incomprehensible to those around him. When he is finally gone, they all weep for different reasons, but none of them are really for him. Little Nicholas cries because he does not understand, the countess and Sonya feel sorry for Natasha, the count knows he will die soon too, and Natasha and Mary are overwhelmed by the mystery of death.

Key Takeaways:

"'Love? What is love?' he thought. 'Love hinders death. Love is life. All, everything that I understand, I understand only because I love. Everything is, everything exists, only because I love. Everything is united by it alone. Love is God, and to die means that I, a particle of love, shall return to the general and eternal source.' These thoughts seemed to him comforting. But they were only thoughts. Something was lacking in them, they were not clear, they were too one-sidedly personal and brain-spun. And there was the former agitation and obscurity. He fell asleep." Andrew has finally experienced love, but he realizes that it is keeping him in this painful limbo between life and death. He falls asleep and realizes that he is not afraid of the mystery. None of the horror of Lise's death and questions of the afterlife can frighten him now.

BOOK THIRTEEN

1812

Book 13: Chapters 1-7

What Happens?

Back at the war front, the Russian troops change position from Ryazan to the Kaluga Road, which is commonly considered an important strategic move in the war, since the Russian forces obtained supplies (and blocked the French from doing so) and managed to separate from the enemy troops who had been trailing them. Tolstoy feels that this interpretation is incorrect and it was mostly luck and the fact that the French troops were disorganized.

Kutuzov knows the French forces are hopelessly wounded, and he intends to wait them out. Napoleon writes to him, hinting that the Russians should surrender—evidently a final effort to save face. Over the next month, the Russian army replenishes while the French army loses its strength.

Emperor Alexander writes to Kutuzov, impatient for him to attack the French. By the time the letter arrives, a battle has already taken place. A Russian soldier rode into the border on the left flank of the French forces, and reported back. Now that their position is known, a battle is inevitable. The date is set for October 5. The day before, one of the generals purposely disappears so orders cannot be delivered to him. On the chosen day, Kutuzov finds that no one is carrying out their orders. The soldiers have been heavily carousing also, and are not in the best shape for battle.

They try again the following day. The battle does not go according to plan because not all communications were received by their intended parties, and it becomes chaotic. However, the battle served its purpose. Although the battle of Tarutino was much smaller than those of Borodino and Austerlitz, it marked the moment when the Russian army shifted from defensive to offensive tactics.

Analysis:

Tolstoy was not afraid to depict the failures of both the French and the Russians. While Pierre's experience in the previous chapters showed the criminal incompetence of the French bureaucracy (including the unjust, clandestine execution), these chapters show the disarray and lack of diligence in the Russian army. Though Kutuzov writes a fine battle plan, it is useless because it is not communicated to the key players. Additionally, the drinking is out of control among the regiments. The Russian army has gained an advantage over the French, but their position is still precarious.

Key Takeaways:

"Just as it is impossible to say when it was decided to abandon Moscow, so it is impossible to say precisely when, or by whom, it was decided to move to Tarutino. Only when the army had got there, as the result of innumerable and varying forces, did people begin to assure themselves that they had desired this movement and long ago foreseen its result." Here Tolstoy adds a new facet to his often-repeated theory of history: those writing history know the conclusion of the events, so they fashion a narrative of intentions leading to that particular outcome.

"'That's how everything is done with us, all topsy-turvy!' said the Russian officers and generals after the Tarutino battle, letting it be understood that some fool there is doing things all wrong but that we ourselves should not have done so, just as people speak today. But people who talk like that either do not know what they are talking about or deliberately deceive themselves. No battle—Tarutino, Borodino, or Austerlitz—takes place as those who planned it anticipated. That is an essential condition. A countless number of free forces (for nowhere is man freer than during a battle, where it is a question of life and death) influence the course taken by the fight, and that course never can be known in advance and never coincides with the direction of any one force." Tolstoy has previously criticized Napoleon's battle plans, but now he contends that battles never go according to plan.

Book 13: Chapters 8-10

What Happens?

After the decisive invasion of Moscow, the French make some poor choices. They fail to establish order in the city—even among their own troops, looting is rampant. Astoundingly, the military commanders never collect winter supplies for the troops. They do not prepare to face the Russians again, even though Kutuzov and his men are at that moment getting ready for future battles.

Instead of preparing the army, Napoleon spends his time in Moscow trying to lure people back to live in the city again. He also tries to reestablish diplomatic relations with Alexander, and at the same time maps out battle possibilities. He enacts severe penalties for looting. None of these plans work, and the city continues burning.

The soldiers are becoming increasingly savage and unprofessional. After the battle of Tarutino, the French troops decide to flee Moscow, but they are heavily loaded down with everything they have plundered. Napoleon allows them to bring everything instead of ordering them to leave it.

Analysis:

As disturbing as these chapters are, Tolstoy emphasizes that it is fear and deprivation that make men behave in such inhuman ways. The soldiers marched for hundreds of miles to get to Moscow, inadequately fed, clothed, or shod. The city held too many allurements. Since looting seemed to be the catalyst for all the other bad behavior among the soldiers, it would make sense for the commanding officers to prevent it, but they cannot. They are trapped in the most vicious of vicious cycles.

Key Takeaways:

"Had Napoleon's aim been to destroy his army, the most skillful strategist could hardly have devised any series of actions that would so completely have accomplished that purpose, independently of anything the Russian army might do.

"Napoleon, the man of genius, did this! But to say that he destroyed his army because he wished to, or because he was very stupid, would be as unjust as to say that he had brought his troops to Moscow because he wished to and because he was very clever and a genius.

"In both cases his personal activity, having no more force than the personal activity of any soldier, merely coincided with the laws that guided the event." In yet another debunking of the "great man" theory, Tolstoy points out that Napoleon's faculties did not deteriorate as a result of his stay in Moscow, but instead he was not in control of the various circumstances and events that led to the weakening of his army once they left the city.

"During the whole of that period Napoleon, who seems to us to have been the leader of all these movements—as the figurehead of a ship may seem to a savage to guide the vessel—acted like a child who, holding a couple of strings inside a carriage, thinks he is driving it."

Book 13: Chapters 11-14

What Happens?

Pierre has thrived in his captive environment. He has prevented a prison riot and won the gratitude of the French officers. He uses his connections to see that others get assistance from their captors. Platon, too, is busy sewing garments for the officers.

The situation changes, though, when the French gather their thirty thousand captives and march them out of the city as prisoners of war. The captors treat them cruelly, and they are unkind to one another. Pierre is placed with the Russian officers, who dislike him because he has avoided them for the whole of his captivity.

The prisoners are disturbed by the extent to which Moscow has been destroyed. They see all of the loot that the French are carrying away, and also observe a wagon full of Russian women who have become army prostitutes.

Analysis:

Pierre has had four weeks with Platon Karataev, who needs very little to be happy. He is a humble, religious person, and his example helps Pierre to endure the atrocities he sees. He knows now that the French, or anyone else, cannot harm his soul, and that is the only thing that matters. If he survives, he will not take any physical comforts for granted again.

Key Takeaways:

"The absence of suffering, the satisfaction of one's needs and consequent freedom in the choice of one's occupation, that is, of one's way of life, now seemed to Pierre to be indubitably man's highest happiness. Here and now for the first time he fully appreciated the enjoyment of eating when he wanted to eat, drinking when he wanted to drink, sleeping when he wanted to sleep, of warmth when he was cold, of talking to a fellow man when he wished to talk and to hear a human voice. The satisfaction of one's needs—good food, cleanliness, and freedom—now that he was deprived of all this, seemed to Pierre to constitute perfect happiness..." Now that Pierre has been separated from all his concerns and comforts, he can understand how to arrange his life. The choice of a profession, over which he agonized once, now seems entirely unimportant in comparison to meeting basic needs.

"All that he now witnessed scarcely made an impression on him—as if his soul, making ready for a hard struggle, refused to receive impressions that might weaken it." His last horrific experience at the execution had nearly broken him mentally. This time, as he walks through the horrors of Moscow, his internal defenses protect him from taking too much in, because it would be more than he could bear.

Book 13: Chapters 15-19

What Happens?

Napoleon writes a letter promising peace (falsely dated from Moscow) to Kutuzov. Many Russian officers want to attack the retreating French, but Kutuzov is reluctant to do so. Finally, the other generals convince him to send a small detachment.

Dokhturov, the leader of the detachment, is an unsung hero in many battles, according to Tolstoy. He delays the attack by sending a messenger to Kutuzov to tell him that the French have retreated from Moscow. Kutuzov is so relieved to hear the news that he weeps and prays in thanksgiving.

He gives orders not to attack the enemy unless it is necessary. The other generals cannot refrain from making some small attacks. The French troops try to firm up their defenses at the same time they try to increase their speed.

Analysis:

Napoleon and Kutuzov are completely different from one another. Even though Napoleon cannot win, he still cannot behave honestly with Kutuzov. The latter, on the other hand, is honest and direct with everyone, and seeks to minimize the senseless losses and suffering of the troops. When he does yield to others, everyone regrets the decision in the end.

Key Takeaways:

"With his sixty years' experience he knew what value to attach to rumors, knew how apt people who desire anything are to group all news so that it appears to confirm what they desire, and he knew how readily in such cases they omit all that makes for the contrary. And the more he desired it the less he allowed himself to believe it. This question absorbed all his mental powers. All else was to him only life's customary routine." So often, the difference between Kutuzov and the other commanders is his experience. They do not yield to the older man's superior experience, so they go out and make the mistakes he tried to prevent.

BOOK FOURTEEN

1812

Book 14: Chapters 1-11

What Happens?

Tolstoy begins the section by explaining how inadequate historical interpretations of the atrocities of war really are, especially in this case. If there were rules for interpreting historical events, it would seem that the French won the Battle of Borodino, since they stayed on the battlefield while the Russians retreated. Guerilla warfare, also known as partisan fighting, also helped the Russians defeat the French. Small groups of fighters, both soldiers disregarding orders and civilians, kept attacking the enemy, slowly chipping away at their strength.

Captain Denisov is now working with one such group of partisans. Dolokhov is about to join him. Their group wants to attack a French transport, but they need more information about it. They take a French drummer boy prisoner, but he cannot tell them anything of value. As they are waiting to raid the transport, Denisov receives a letter, delivered by Petya Rostov. Against direct orders from his general, Petya decides to stay and join the raid.

Denisov sends Tikhon, a peasant partisan, ahead of the group to find out how many guards are protecting the transport. The French see Tikhon and open fire. He manages to return to Denisov's camp. He took a prisoner but did not bring him back, and saw enough about the transport to plan the attack.

Petya tries his hardest to appear like an adult. Dolokhov arrives with French uniforms in hand, planning to do reconnaissance in disguise. He gives the second uniform to Petya, and they enter the French camp, posing as officers. Speaking in flawless French, Dolokhov asks the officers for various details. The officers are suspicious, and Petya is petrified with fear. Nevertheless, they are allowed to leave.

Petya cannot sleep the night before the attack, and stays up talking with Cossacks and listening to their music. Petya, as everyone feared, behaves recklessly in the attack and is shot in the head. Denisov is devastated at the boy's death; Dolokhov acts indifferent. The partisan group rescues some Russian prisoners, including Pierre.

Analysis:

Although in other places Tolstoy idealizes simple peasant life (or at least strongly prefers it to "civilized" high society), the incident in which Tikhon kills the man he was supposed to bring back as a prisoner shows that a peasant can be cruel and callous in the face of death. Then again, so is Dolokhov, who is not a peasant. These men, who can be so blasé about death and killing, contrast the naiveté of Petya.

We have seen combat through the eyes of Nicholas Rostov, Andrew Bolkonski, and Pierre Bezukhov. All of them become disillusioned as time goes on; all have near misses with death. For one final scene of the atrocities of war, we watch as Petya experiences war like the child he is, and a bullet finds him easily.

Key Takeaways:

"He tried to remember whether he had not done anything else that was foolish. And running over the events of the day he remembered the French drummer boy. 'It's capital for us here, but what of him? Where have they put him? Have they fed him? Haven't they hurt his feelings?' he thought. But having caught himself saying too much about the flints, he was now afraid to speak out.

"'I might ask,' he thought, 'but they'll say: "He's a boy himself and so he pities the boy." I'll show them tomorrow whether I'm a boy. Will it seem odd if I ask?' Petya thought. 'Well, never mind!' and immediately, blushing and looking anxiously at the officers to see if they appeared ironical, he said:

"'May I call in that boy who was taken prisoner and give him something to eat?... Perhaps...'

"'Yes, he's a poor little fellow,' said Denisov, who evidently saw nothing shameful in this reminder. 'Call him in. His name is Vincent Bosse. Have him fetched.'" Petya shows his typical Rostov hospitality and generosity—he treats even the prisoner of war like a guest.

Book 14: Chapters 12-15

What Happens?

Returning to Pierre's story, no other orders had been given regarding the prisoners of war since they had left Moscow, marching with the retreating French army. Half of the wagons with which they had left Moscow had been captured. Many of the soldiers are deserting. The prisoners' numbers have been reduced to less than a third of what they had been on leaving Moscow; they keep falling ill and/or getting shot.

Platon Karataev falls ill with a fever, and Pierre distances himself from his friend, knowing what will happen. He allows Platon to tell him a story he has heard several times before, about a man falsely convicted of murder. The man is sentenced to hard labor, but accepts his lot because he has committed other smaller sins in his life. The real murderer is serving out a sentence there, too, and tells the warden of the first man's innocence. A letter is sent to the tsar, who pardons the man, but by this time the man has died. Platon's point is that he received the only forgiveness that mattered—God's—and that death is part of that.

Platon grows too sick to march, so he allows the soldiers to shoot him. Pierre avoids being with him when he is shot, for which he feels guilty. That night he dreams of his old geography teacher, who lectures him about Platon's death. As he wakes up, Denisov's men have arrived to rescue the prisoners.

Analysis:

The story Platon tells is actually one that Tolstoy had published earlier on its own. The questions of innocence, sin, and forgiveness are ones that Tolstoy wrestled with for all of his life, and his theories on the subject influenced many great thinkers, including Ernest Hemingway, Mohandas K. Gandhi, and Martin Luther King, Jr. Its placement here in the story is significant, as Pierre will have to understand forgiveness to truly become a whole person.

Key Takeaways:

"'Life is everything. Life is God. Everything changes and moves and that movement is God. And while there is life there is joy in consciousness of the divine. To love life is to love God. Harder and more blessed than all else is to love this life in one's sufferings, in innocent sufferings.'

"'Karataev!' came to Pierre's mind.

"And suddenly he saw vividly before him a long-forgotten, kindly old man who had given him geography lessons in Switzerland. 'Wait a bit,' said the old man, and showed Pierre a globe. This globe was alive—a vibrating ball without fixed dimensions. Its whole surface consisted of drops closely pressed together, and all these drops moved and changed places, sometimes several of them merging into one, sometimes one dividing into many. Each drop tried to spread out and occupy as much space as possible, but others striving to do the same compressed it, sometimes destroyed it, and sometimes merged with it.

"'That is life,' said the old teacher.

"'How simple and clear it is,' thought Pierre. 'How is it I did not know it before?'

"'God is in the midst, and each drop tries to expand so as to reflect Him to the greatest extent. And it grows, merges, disappears from the surface, sinks to the depths, and again emerges. There now, Karataev has spread out and disappeared. Do you understand, my child?' said the teacher.

"'Do you understand, damn you?' shouted a voice, and Pierre woke up." This highly symbolic dream in which Pierre can come to terms with Platon's death gives way to the reality of a soldier shouting at Pierre to wake him up. This is not intended as a comic moment so much as it is an illustration of Tolstoy's belief that the dreams a person remembers are always the ones right before he wakes up, and usually incorporate some of the sensory input a person is starting to experience as he is waking.

Book 14: Chapters 16-19

What Happens?

The war was incredibly costly for both sides, Tolstoy reminds us yet again. The French army had started out with four hundred thousand soldiers from all over the Empire; they left Moscow with seventy-three thousand men; they are now down to thirty-six thousand. They finally arrive at Smolensk, in terrible condition and low spirits.

Finding yet another way to illustrate the war, Tolstoy compares the Russians' pursuit of the French as they retreated to a game of blind man's bluff. Russian troops keep taking the opportunity to attack, even though Kutuzov feels that it is wrong in principle to attack an army that is already retreating. This forces the French to be even more frantic in their rush to leave Russia. Their leader, Napoleon, escapes faster than anyone.

Despite what historians like to claim, Napoleon's retreat was not glorious, and Russia's seeming victory was Pyrrhic as well. There was no planning, no strategy, on the part of the French. The Russians caused themselves huge losses in their relentless pursuit of the retreating army.

Analysis:

In case it had not been apparent throughout the novel, the author was a pacifist, and in these chapters he states plainly that the war was not worth the cost. Any attempts to frame it in the context of national glory (for Russia or France) are false, in his opinion. This section of the book is bookended by strongly worded historical essays; the examples from history are integrated into the author's philosophy. There can be no questioning how the author feels or why he was motivated to create such a long, complex book.

Key Takeaways:

"After staggering into Smolensk which seemed to them a promised land, the French, searching for food, killed one another, sacked their own stores, and when everything had been plundered fled farther. They all went without knowing whither or why they were going. Still less did that genius, Napoleon, know it, for no one issued any orders to him. But still he and those about him retained their old habits: wrote commands, letters, reports, and orders of the day; called one another sire, mon cousin, prince d'Eckmuhl, roi de Naples, and so on. But these orders and reports were only on paper, nothing in them was acted upon for they could not be carried out, and though they entitled one another Majesties, Highnesses, or Cousins, they all felt that they were miserable wretches who had done much evil for which they had now to pay. And though they pretended to be concerned about the army, each was thinking only of himself and of how to get away quickly and save himself." Tolstoy loves to sarcastically call Napoleon a "genius." His contempt for him here is especially great, since Napoleon leaves his troops so that he can escape quickly out of Russia.

"'C'est grand!'* say the historians, and there no longer exists either good or evil but only 'grand' and 'not grand.' Grand is good, not grand is bad. Grand is the characteristic, in their conception, of some special animals called 'heroes.' And Napoleon, escaping home in a warm fur coat and leaving to perish those who were not merely his comrades but were (in his opinion) men he had brought there, feels que c'est grand,*[2] and his soul is tranquil.

* 'It is great.'

*[2] That it is great.

'Du sublime (he saw something sublime in himself) au ridicule il n'y a qu'un pas,'* said he. And the whole world for fifty years has been repeating: 'Sublime! Grand! Napoleon le Grand!' Du sublime au ridicule il n'y a qu'un pas.

*'From the sublime to the ridiculous is but a step.'

"And it occurs to no one that to admit a greatness not commensurable with the standard of right and wrong is merely to admit one's own nothingness and immeasurable meanness.

"For us with the standard of good and evil given us by Christ, no human actions are incommensurable. And there is no greatness where simplicity, goodness, and truth are absent." Tolstoy is determined to correct this lingering perception that Napoleon was a "great man;" he sees nothing great about someone acting like a selfish coward.

"The people had a single aim: to free their land from invasion. That aim was attained in the first place of itself, as the French ran away, and so it was only necessary not to stop their flight. Secondly it was attained by the guerrilla warfare which was destroying the French, and thirdly by the fact that a large Russian army was following the French, ready to use its strength in case their movement stopped.

The Russian army had to act like a whip to a running animal. And the experienced driver knew it was better to hold the whip raised as a menace than to strike the running animal on the head." This image of whipping a running animal is a powerful one: Russia could have merely stopped whipping, and the animal still would have run away.

BOOK FIFTEEN

1812-1813

Book 15: Chapters 1-3

What Happens?

Natasha and Mary draw closer as they mourn Andrew's death. Mary realizes that she has to take care of Andrew's son, so she begins putting a life together, for Natasha plans to move back to Moscow with Mary when she receives a letter with the news of Petya's death.

Countess Rostov becomes hysterical when she learns that her youngest son has been killed. She is in complete denial. Natasha stays with her for three weeks, gradually helping her to return to reality and begin to grieve.

Grief causes Countess Rostov's health to worsen dramatically. As Natasha cares for her mother, she finds that it rejuvenates her, and she develops a close friendship with Princess Mary over their mutual grief for Andrew.

Analysis:

While the Rostovs have always seemed superior to many of the other characters for their truly loving spirit, this section shows that they lack balance. In contrast, Mary is grief-stricken over her brother (and still wrestling with guilt and grief over her father's death), but she is a more practical person. She does not allow her grief to keep her from fulfilling her obligations to others. The countess, on the other hand, cannot function, and imposes her emotions on Natasha. The latter cannot leave, in fact, because her mother's feelings dictate that no one else can substitute for her.

Key Takeaways:

"The mother's wounded spirit could not heal. Petya's death had torn from her half her life. When the news of Petya's death had come she had been a fresh and vigorous woman of fifty, but a month later she left her room a listless old woman taking no interest in life. But the same blow that almost killed the countess, this second blow, restored Natasha to life." Countess Rostova's journey in *War and Peace* has been a difficult one. She and her husband are generous, helpful people, but not good at managing their money. Bad luck, bad decisions, and the crisis of war have cost them their fortune and property; now the war has cost them their son.

Book 15: Chapters 4-11

What Happens?

The winter is just as cold for the Russian soldiers as it is for the French. They are every bit as exhausted. Kutuzov knows this, so he slows down the speed of the pursuit. They need to rest and prepare for one last battle at the town of Krasnoe. He regrets the conditions in which his men and the French prisoners of war must live.

The morale is high as the soldiers easily defeat some French forces. Kutuzov makes a speech calling for some compassion for the prisoners they have taken, most of whom are in terrible condition from frostbite. He also talks about Napoleon with some salty language, causing the soldiers to cheer.

As the soldiers sit around a campfire one night, two deserting French soldiers come to the camp to surrender themselves because they will otherwise soon die of exposure to the cold. The Frenchmen turn out to be Captain Ramballe and his orderly. Ramballe must be carried to a tent. The orderly makes friends with the Russians by trying to teach them French songs.

The Russian army implements a pointless (in Tolstoy's view) plan to move ahead of the French and trap Napoleon at the Berezina River. The plan fails, and the other military personnel ensure that Kutuzov is blamed for the failure, though he had opposed the scheme all along. Kutuzov is falling into disfavor with the Emperor, who wants the army to pursue the French past the Russian border. Kutuzov knows that there would be no benefit to this, and that his men are not equipped for it. He receives orders to step down. Kutuzov is awarded Russia's highest military honor, the Order of St. George, and retires to private life in Vilna. He dies soon after this.

Analysis:

This section of the book serves as a kind of eulogy for Kutuzov. Tolstoy repeatedly shows Kutuzov's good leadership in action—and also shows the treachery going on behind the scenes, as younger men pin the blame for their mistakes on the placid, pious old man who they know will not retaliate. Tolstoy wants to rehabilitate the image of Kutuzov just as much as he wants to debunk the myth that Napoleon was a "great man." In fact, if anyone is a "great man" in Tolstoy's estimation, it is Kutuzov. The old general always acts in a wise and compassionate way; by preventing countless calamities, he has probably greatly changed the course of history for the better, but does not get credit for it.

Key Takeaways:

"They blamed Kutuzov and said that from the very beginning of the campaign he had prevented their vanquishing Napoleon, that he thought of nothing but satisfying his passions and would not advance from the Linen Factories because he was comfortable there, that at Krasnoe he checked the advance because on learning that Napoleon was there he had quite lost his head, and that it was probable that he had an understanding with Napoleon and had been bribed by him, and so on, and so on.

"Not only did his contemporaries, carried away by their passions, talk in this way, but posterity and history have acclaimed Napoleon as grand, while Kutuzov is described by foreigners as a crafty, dissolute, weak old courtier, and by Russians as something indefinite- a sort of puppet useful only because he had a Russian name." One of the main missions Tolstoy had in writing *War and Peace* was to rehabilitate the image of Kutuzov. While the latter made some unpopular choices, his motivation was always to preserve his troops. Without him, many of the battles would have had quite a different outcome.

Book 15: Chapters 12-20

What Happens?

Pierre sees the body of Petya Rostov, and at last learns from Denisov that his wife had died, and that Andrew died a month after the battle of Borodino. Pierre falls ill, but recovers, and has a new perspective on the meaning of life. He has lost much of his wealth, but he chooses to repay his wife's debts anyway.

Pierre returns to Moscow after he recuperates. He visits Natasha and Mary, and they discuss their experiences during the war. He emphasizes the moral lessons that he gained from his captivity.

Pierre is still in love with Natasha. He asks Mary to help him propose marriage to her. He eventually works up the courage to speak to her of his love, which she returns, and they agree to marry.

Analysis:

Mary's tendency to harbor guilt knows no bounds. While initially she was glad to think that Pierre and Natasha might find happiness together, she is struck with the guilty feeling that she and they are forgetting Andrew too soon. Just as with her father's death, she was not willing to accept her father's attempt at reconciliation as "enough," so too here she overthinks the process of mourning.

Pierre and Natasha's romance springs up at nearly the very end of the novel, yet it has been building for the entire time. Their relationships with others had been full of strife, causing them to harm themselves and others, but this relationship is different. They are at peace with themselves and with one another.

Key Takeaways:

"It would be difficult to explain why and whither ants whose heap has been destroyed are hurrying: some from the heap dragging bits of rubbish, larvae, and corpses, others back to the heap, or why they jostle, overtake one another, and fight, and it would be equally difficult to explain what caused the Russians after the departure of the French to throng to the place that had formerly been Moscow. But when we watch the ants round their ruined heap, the tenacity, energy, and immense number of the delving insects prove that despite the destruction of the heap, something indestructible, which though intangible is the real strength of the colony, still exists; and similarly, though in Moscow in the month of October there was no government and no churches, shrines, riches, or houses—it was still the Moscow it had been in August. All was destroyed, except something intangible yet powerful and indestructible." Again the condition of Moscow seems to parallel the surviving characters' inner lives, particularly Pierre, Natasha and Mary. They have suffered huge, painful losses but are ready to rebuild.

"He told of his adventures as he had never yet recalled them. He now, as it were, saw a new meaning in all he had gone through. Now that he was telling it all to Natasha he experienced that pleasure which a man has when women listen to him—not clever women who when listening either try to remember what they hear to enrich their minds and when opportunity offers to retell it, or who wish to adopt it to some thought of their own and promptly contribute their own clever comments prepared in their little mental workshop—but the pleasure given by real women gifted with a capacity to select and absorb the very best a man shows of himself. Natasha without knowing it was all attention: she did not lose a word, no single quiver in Pierre's voice, no look, no twitch of a muscle in his face, nor a single gesture. She caught the unfinished word in its flight and took it straight into her open heart, divining the secret meaning of all Pierre's mental travail." Talking to Natasha helps Pierre to find meaning in his experience, and, ultimately, his existence. Unlike his marriage to Helene, which drove him further into selfishness and depression, his second marriage will bring out the better qualities in him.

FIRST EPILOGUE 1813-1820

What Happens?

After two chapters discussing Alexander I and Napoleon, Tolstoy continues the story of the families in the novel. Pierre and Natasha get married, and Count Ilya Rostov dies soon after. The countess's physical and mental health is failing, and the estate is on the verge of bankruptcy. Nicholas comes home to manage the estate, pay off the debts, and take care of everyone. He is miserable because he wants to marry Mary Bolkonskaya, but thinks that his poverty makes that impossible. Mary, though, does not mind, and her fortune saves the Rostov family.

Nicholas grows successful at managing the estate. He learns about the technical aspects of agriculture, and he also learns how to treat his serfs well so that they are productive and content. Nicholas and Mary have a strong marriage, as do Pierre and Natasha, and the epilogue depicts how they handle disagreements and parenting concerns.

At the end, Pierre and Nicholas argue about how Emperor Alexander has lost himself in religious fervor and has left the country in the hands of dangerous people. Pierre favors some kind of change, but Nicholas supports the Emperor. The end shows young Nicholas (Andrew's son) contemplating doing something great with his life. He also greatly admires Pierre. Many readers believe that Tolstoy is hinting that Pierre and young Nicholas will take part in the Decembrist uprising in 1825, which was a failed attempt to assassinate the Emperor.

Tolstoy pauses for another critical essay of the "great man" theory of history. He argues that broader circumstances, caused by an infinite number of small decisions, actually cause major historical events. He tells Napoleon's life story and explains how its events were not driven by the Emperor, but by external circumstances.

Analysis:

Tolstoy's epilogue to *War and Peace* is another innovation in storytelling: an epilogue normally provides closure to the main story, but this epilogue raises more new questions rather than resolving old ones. Tolstoy acknowledges that the 19th century will be full of upheavals, and how that will affect these characters, most of whom are still quite young.

War and Peace has chronicled the development of Pierre, from a foreign-raised atheist to a cuckolded husband to an ardent, if ineffectual, believer, to a balanced, authentic person. He still belongs to the Freemasons, but understands that there are many ways to change one's life and surroundings for the better.

Natasha, too, has changed. We met her as an emotional little girl, and watched her transition from a naïve flirt to a somber, religious young woman. In the end, she is barely recognizable as a matronly mother of four. Pierre and Natasha have an honest, drama-free marriage, because they have both already endured so much to become who they are. Their love is based on friendship and moral principles.

Key Takeaways:

"He had dreamed that he and Uncle Pierre, wearing helmets such as were depicted in his Plutarch, were leading a huge army. The army was made up of white slanting lines that filled the air like the cobwebs that float about in autumn and which Dessalles called les fils de la Vierge. In front was Glory, which was similar to those threads but rather thicker. He and Pierre were borne along lightly and joyously, nearer and nearer to their goal. Suddenly the threads that moved them began to slacken and become entangled and it grew difficult to move. And Uncle Nicholas stood before them in a stern and threatening attitude." The first epilogue, and last scene of the characters, ends with a dream. Reminiscent of the many other important dreams featured in the book, this dream features easily accessible symbols: Nicholas and Pierre become entangled with politics. Nicholas wakes and feels that his father must have sent him the dream, and vows to make him proud.

SECOND EPILOGUE

What Happens?

Tolstoy discusses some of the themes of the book, such as the "great man" theory and the nature of human reason and free will. The author advises historians to consider events in the context of all the other events that came before. He also argues that even the lowliest people influence history, not just the great ones.

At some length, Tolstoy discusses the relationship between the course of a nation and the lives of the individuals within. The question is whether people have free will if history is predestined. The author believes that the tension between freedom and historical predestination ("necessity") is resolved by God. Individual freedom is the ultimate force that drives human history. There is no contradiction, Tolstoy says; necessity follows from freedom.

Analysis:

Tolstoy's sophisticated essays in this section are some of the most challenging parts of the novel, and some translations even omit them. However, they help tie the book's numerous plots and subplots together. *War and Peace's* many interwoven stories of military and home life all illustrate the relationship between individual free will and historical necessity.

Key Takeaways:

"The problem is that regarding man as a subject of observation from whatever point of view—theological, historical, ethical, or philosophic—we find a general law of necessity to which he (like all that exists) is subject. But regarding him from within ourselves as what we are conscious of, we feel ourselves to be free.

"This consciousness is a source of self-cognition quite apart from and independent of reason.

"Through his reason man observes himself, but only through consciousness does he know himself. Apart from consciousness of self no observation or application of reason is conceivable." In the end, the aim of history is to make sense of human beings, who are not always sensible or rational. It requires a multifaceted approach to take in the whole picture, one that is both broad and contextualized, and also individual and personal. These are the very tactics used to write *War and Peace.*

Character List

(In order of importance and then appearance)

Count Peter (Pierre) Kirilovich Bezukhov: Awkward, stout, bespectacled, and mild, Pierre has a hard time fitting into high society. His good nature endears him to his elderly father, so that he bestows his title and fortune on this son born out of wedlock. He is close friends with Andrew Bolkonski and the Rostov family. After a brief acquaintance, he marries Helene Kuragina, and their marriage is troubled from the start. Pierre's spiritual journey from atheism to Freemasonry to selfless love forms the core of the novel.

Countess Natalia (Natasha) Ilyinichna Rostova: The third of four children in the Rostov family, Natasha first appears in the novel as a twelve-year-old girl just on the verge of growing up. She still carries a doll, but she is also experiencing her first romantic feelings toward her relative, Boris Drubetskoy. Even at this young age, she has such vitality, honesty, and love of beauty that set her apart from the other girls. As the years pass, she falls in love many times, and suffers major setbacks. She grows from a flirtatious debutante to a woman of substance.

Prince Andrew Nikolayevich Bolkonski: Pierre's friend Andrew appears in the novel almost immediately. Intelligent, bold, and at times arrogant, he is Pierre's opposite. Unhappily married to Lise, he goes to war in 1805, and it seems he will have a brilliant military career. Then he gets injured, his wife dies in childbirth, and he retires to private life for several years. Finally, the war situation becomes so dire that he is drawn back into government service. He and Natasha Rostova become engaged, but the engagement is broken off when Natasha plans to elope with Anatole Kuragin. Andrew goes to the war front and is injured at the battle of Borodino.

Princess Mary Nikolayevna Bolkonskaya: Andrew's sister, Mary, has not been as fortunate as he has in escaping from their domineering father. Prince Nicholas Bolkonski verbally abuses Mary as he tries to teach her mathematics and science. He mocks her sincere religious devotion. Mary's life is a lonely one at the family estate, Bald Hills, where her only friends are her female companion, Mademoiselle Bourienne, her old nurse, and the religious pilgrims who visit her. Since the family is wealthy, several young men are considering marrying Mary for her money. She plans to remain single and go on a pilgrimage, but the war and her family obligations prevent her from doing so—and then she meets Nicholas Rostov.

Prince Nicholas Andreevich Bolkonski: Andrew and Mary's father, the elderly Prince Nicholas, is a famous general who served under Catherine the Great. He has tried to rule over his family and estate, Bald Hills, the way he did his regiments. As he ages, he becomes more cantankerous and cruel to his family, particularly his daughter, Mary. Yet, despite his advanced age and increasing senility, he finds himself in charge of the war effort in his region, and the activity seems to prolong his life. Finally, as Napoleon's troops are about to invade his ancestral estate, he suffers two strokes and dies, as a kind of symbol of the end of the old era of history.

Count Nicholas Ilyich Rostov: Natasha's brother, Nicholas, insists on joining the military in 1805, where he serves as a hussar, or light-cavalry officer. He grows from being a frightened novice on the battlefield to an experienced, wise soldier. He and Sonya Rostova, his penniless cousin, are childhood sweethearts, but as the family's finances decline, and as Nicholas matures, it becomes clear that he must marry someone else. He exacerbates the financial problems by gambling: he loses forty-three thousand rubles to Dolokhov, a mercenary officer who leads several of the protagonists into wrongdoing.

Princess Elena (Helene) Vasilyevna Kuragina: Pierre's first wife, Helene, is stunningly beautiful and skilled at social maneuvering, but she has no morals. She marries Pierre for his money and prestige, but expects to keep entertaining the attentions of other men. At first, the nature of these other relationships is not clear—Pierre fights a duel with Dolokhov on suspicion alone. Eventually, her affairs with other men are common knowledge. Pierre separates from her for a time, but eventually reconciles with her to a limited extent. She tries to divorce him to marry someone else, but dies, it is hinted, as a result of an attempted abortion.

Prince Anatole Vasilyevich Kuragin: It is rumored that Helene has an incestuous relationship with her brother, Anatole. This rumor is never confirmed, but like Helene, Anatole is extremely good-looking and amoral. He and Dolokhov are Pierre's drinking buddies, getting him into trouble with the law, and damaging his reputation in society. Later, Anatole tries to seduce Natasha while she is engaged to Andrew Bolkonski. Natasha is so destroyed by her mistake with Anatole that she tries to poison herself. Anatole serves with the army as a way to avoid the consequences of his actions; Andrew Bolkonski keeps following him to challenge him to a duel.

Fyodor Ivanovich Dolokhov: Dolokhov is one of the common threads that run through many of the characters' stories. He first appears in the novel as one of the friends who draws Pierre into drinking and debauchery. Then he appears at the war front, chatting with the enemy before the battle, and trying to distinguish himself in front of General Kutuzov. Pierre challenges him to a duel over his "friendship" with Helene, and Dolokhov is wounded. It is then we learn that he adores his mother and sister, both of whom are poor and sickly. Later he falls in love with Sonya Rostova, and when she rejects him, he punishes Nicholas for it by winning it back at cards.

General Mikhail Ilarionovich Kutuzov: An elderly general, Kutuzov has led a long and distinguished career. His primary concern is to save his troops: by sparing them from unnecessary fighting, marching, and deprivation, they will be better prepared to win future battles. No other commander sees the situation the same way, and they sometimes work against Kutuzov. His humility and spirituality stand out in sharp contrast to the other self-serving military men, and even sharper contrast to the egomaniac Napoleon. Eventually, Kutuzov falls from favor over some of his decisions, though they probably saved thousands of lives.

Napoleon I of France: Emperor of France from 1804 to 1815, Napoleon's military aggressions cause the wars depicted in *War and Peace*. He appears in the novel as a developed character, not merely a villain or a "great man." He is a complex person who can be both compassionate and ruthless, cordial and rude, a master strategist who still makes some major mistakes. Early in the novel, Pierre and Andrew had idolized Napoleon. Over time, though, both of them come to see his shortcomings as a leader.

Emperor Alexander I of Russia: Emperor of Russia from 1801-1825, Alexander was an enigmatic ruler who inspired deep devotion in his subjects. In the novel, he induces a patriotic fervor in many characters, including Nicholas and Petya Rostov. He appears in the novel both on the battlefield and at grand society events, and is always shown to be a sensitive, thoughtful person. At the same time, though, he is a bit too sensitive, not able to stomach the terrible battles, and far too trusting of Napoleon. He also loses patience with his military commanders, particularly Kutuzov, though the latter is far wiser and a more experienced strategist.

Prince Boris Drubetskoy: A relative of the Rostovs whom they took in and educated with their own children. Boris and his mother are impoverished and dependent on the kindness of others to stay afloat in aristocratic society. His mother calls in favors and borrows money to get him started in military service. He takes it upon himself to rise in society through connections and hard work. He marries for money, though he had twice been in love with Natasha.

Sofia Alexandrovna (Sonya) Rostova: Sonya is the orphaned niece of the Rostovs, and they also raised her with their own children. She is Natasha's best friend, and is much quieter than her cousin. She and Nicholas were childhood sweethearts who renew their love after he returns from military service on leave, but the family opposes their marriage. Sonya desperately tries to hold on to Nicholas, but eventually she accepts that he must marry another.

Anna Pavlovna Scherer: A forty-year-old spinster, Anna is one of the key figures in Petersburg society. She is a close friend of the royal family, and her parties bring together many fashionable people. Her inappropriate matchmaking attempts and her continued friendship with immoral people like Helene Bezukhova would suggest Anna's own character is questionable. Yet we also see her positive qualities, such as the way she treats her elderly aunt with care and respect.

Count Ilya Rostov: Count Rostov, the patriarch of the Rostov family, is fun-loving and generous to a fault. He also holds to a high code of honor. When Nicholas loses forty-three thousand rubles gambling with Dolokhov, his father raises the money to pay him back, even if Dolokhov had not seriously intended to obtain such a large sum from Nicholas.

Countess Natalia Rostova: The countess has more instincts for self-preservation and protection of the children than her husband does, but she is also a generous, hospitable person. She is a person who believes in following rules and social norm, and cannot understand her daughter Natasha's wild imagination.

Vera Rostova Berg: The eldest Rostov daughter, Vera is attractive, intelligent, and principled, but she has none of the endearing qualities of her sister, Natasha. When she first appears in the novel, she tattles on the other children to their parents. As the years pass, she changes in circumstance, but not in essence. She has the habit of asking people embarrassing, overly personal questions. She marries Berg, and together they obsess over how to succeed in society.

Alphonse Karlovich Berg: A German-born officer of a respectable background, Berg is socially ambitious and determined. He sees Vera Rostova and immediately decides he will marry her, though his plan takes several years to execute. He works his way up in the military, and her family's finances are in steep decline, so that when he asks her father for her hand, he is successful because there were no other suitors. He presses Count Rostov for a sizable dowry, and ends up taking a promissory note for most of it. He is materialistic, unimaginative, and nearly emotionless—but so is Vera, so they are quite compatible.

Pyotr Ilyich (Petya) Rostov: The youngest member of the Rostov family, Petya has the ability to make the other family members cheerful. He insists upon enlisting in the war at age fifteen, and his parents struggle to find a way that will fulfill his wish along with their need to protect him.

Anna Mikhaylovna Drubetskaya: The enterprising mother of Boris, Anna Mikhaylovna lives to try to make her son's life better. She has a great deal of skill at maneuvering people and events to get what she wants. She helps prevent Pierre's relatives from stealing his inheritance—a favor she expects will be repaid by some financial assistance to Boris.

Vasili (Vaska) Denisov: A Russian military officer, Denisov is a close friend of Nicholas Rostov's for most of his military career. He has a speech impediment and Tolstoy tends to spell out his pronunciations phonetically. He is from a lower social class than the Rostovs, but when he comes home on leave with Nicholas, he falls in love with Natasha and proposes without talking to her parents first. He sometimes bends the rules to take care of his men. Eventually he becomes a leader of partisan troops during the French retreat.

Joseph Bazdeev: Joseph Bazdeev is the mysterious stranger who finds Pierre at a low moment in his life and recruits him into Freemasonry. He is sincere in his beliefs. Pierre is won over by his erudition and insightfulness, but later learns that most Freemasons are not like him.

Platon Karataev: The humble, kind peasant who befriends Pierre while both are imprisoned during the occupation of Moscow, Platon Karataev needs very little to be happy. His example teaches Pierre how to have a reasonable outlook on life.

Themes in the Book

History: *War and Peace* was intended to be a new kind of history: historical fiction, with invented characters and real historical figures taking part in events that actually happened. Moreover, Tolstoy wanted to show the defects and limitations of history, and often philosophizes about historians and their work.

Rationality vs. Irrationality: Although wars are fought with deliberate strategies, the novel explores the many ways in which human beings act irrationally in war and in peace, and how wisdom can transcend both logic and emotion. Frequently, this theme takes the form of the irrational feelings of love and/or lust that cause many characters to act in dangerous and detrimental ways.

The "Great Man" Theory: Although *War and Peace* is set in the years 1805-1813, it was written in the 1860s—a time of intense philosophical debate, which deeply influenced Tolstoy's writing. In the 1840s, Scottish writer Thomas Carlyle had introduced his theory that history can be explained in terms of the actions of a few exceptionally talented heroes, or "great men." Over the next two decades, this idea was debated and expanded, and in 1860 Herbert Spencer posed the counterargument that such great men were the products of the societies into which they were born, whose social conditions had formed long before these men were born. Napoleon Bonaparte, a well-known example of a "great man," appears in *War and Peace* to affirm Spencer's argument; at the same time, one could argue, Tolstoy's depiction of General Kutuzov lends some support to the original "great man" theory.

The Search for the Meaning of Life and Death: Many of the younger characters are searching for the purpose and meaning of their lives, and do not have peace with themselves or others until they find what they are seeking. Yet, as important as this search is, the author constantly shows lives ending—at all ages—showing that life is fleeting, and that assigning meaning to it does not add length to one's life.

Family Ties: The novel tells the story of five aristocratic families—the Bezukhovs, the Bolkonskis, the Rostovs, the Kuragins and the Drubetskoys—whose lives are entangled both with the other families as well as with the historical events taking place in the early 19th century, which are, of course, partly the result of the interactions of the royal families of Europe. The actions of the parents in *War and Peace* often have profound effects on their children, causing both positive and negative outcomes.

The True Nature of Russia: Like many thinkers of the 1860s, Tolstoy was obsessed with ideas about what Russia is and what it means to be Russian—and what it is not. There were two schools of thought at the time, and Tolstoy gives space to ideas from both of them. On the one hand, there were Slavophiles who believed that Russia's roots were connected to its pre-Christian, nature-worshipping, Asian-influenced heritage. On the other hand, the Westernizers felt that Russia was not only part of Europe, but actually could be the savior of it, especially when upstarts like Napoleon dared to challenge the Tsar (now called an Emperor), who was thought to have inherited the divine right to rule.

Faith and Morality: Throughout the novel, we see many forms of religious faith (and lack of it). From the Russian Orthodox rites of baptism to death vigils, to Pierre's atheism, his Freemasonry, and Mary's religious pilgrims, motifs of faith constantly appear in the novel. Additionally, there are many moral questions and issues in the lives of the characters that intersect with practices of faith in interesting ways. Forgiveness is an important component of many of these questions of faith and morality.

About The Book

In Russian, the language in which it was originally written, *War and Peace* is called *Voyna i mir*; the title is slightly ambiguous, since it could also mean "War and the World" and there do exist proponents of that theory; however, since Tolstoy met the French pacifist author Pierre-Joseph Proudhon in Europe and greatly admired him, it seems most likely that the title is a tribute to Proudhon's work *La Guerre et la Paix* (meaning "*War and Peace*" in French). The author's name is Count Lev Nikolayevich Tolstoy, but his given name is usually Anglicized to Leo.

War and Peace defies easy categorization. One person might say that its genre is historical fiction, another might call it an epic saga, a third might say it is a realistic novel; none of them would be incorrect. Written from 1863-'69 and published serially from 1865 to 1869, the story begins in July 1805 and follows its characters through the 1812 French invasion, the battles of Borodino and Tarutino, and the occupation of Moscow, all the way to the French retreat and the rebuilding of Russia. The first half of the book was published in the magazine *The Russian Messenger* under the title *The Year 1805*. Eventually, the whole novel was published as a four-volume set.

An unnamed, omniscient, third-person narrator recounts the facts and inner thoughts of the characters. The narrator also provides historical facts, and presents philosophical discourses with increasing frequency as the book progresses. Finally, the second epilogue consists only of philosophy and analysis of history. The novel is written in the past tense, looking back on the events of 1805-1812 from some distance.

The book has a variety of settings in Russia and Eastern Europe, including St. Petersburg, Moscow, and the Russian countryside, and the war fronts in Austria and Prussia. While there are approximately 580 characters, the main protagonists are generally considered to be Pierre Bezukhov, Andrew Bolkonski, Natasha Rostova, Mary Bolkonskaya, Nicholas Rostov, and General Kutuzov.

Originally, Tolstoy's novel was going to be about the Decembrist uprising in 1825, when a group of young aristocrats attempted to assassinate Emperor Alexander. While conducting research about the uprising, Tolstoy developed an interest in Napoleon's campaign, and the seeds for *War and Peace* were planted in his mind. Tolstoy was not content to read others' descriptions of the Napoleonic Wars; to write accurately about the battle scenes, he visited the sites in person with surveyors' tools in hand. Interestingly, the action of *War and Peace* ends in 1820, and depicts some characters feeling discontent toward Emperor Alexander, so the story ends up in nearly the place that the author began.

The immediate response to *War and Peace* was positive. The public enjoyed reading it, and many scholars wrote reviews and essays based on it. Among those who disliked the book, some critics felt confused by the mixing of historical and fictional elements, and others felt that it was not critical enough of the old nobility and the social problems that existed at that time. Nevertheless, the popularity and acclaim of the book led to translations into many languages, and adaptations into film, opera, theater, radio, and television have been made.

About The Author

Count Lev Nikolayevich Tolstoy was born on his family estate in Central Russia, Yasnaya Polyana, in 1828. The Tolstoys were an aristocratic family who could trace their lineage back for centuries. He was the fourth of five children born to Count Nikolay Ilyich Tolstoy, who was a veteran of the War of 1812. Orphaned at a young age, he and his siblings were brought up by relatives. Lev studied the law but failed to earn a degree at the University of Kazan. Rich and idle, he spent the next several years engaged in drinking, gambling, and debauchery, until he eventually joined an artillery regiment in the Caucasus in 1851. He began writing in earnest as he fought in the Crimean War, and the results were eventually published as *Sebastopol Sketches,* which brought him some success in the literary world. He lived for some time in St. Petersburg and also made two lengthy trips to Europe, where he had some of the most important experiences of his life. He met some of the authors he respected most, including Victor Hugo and Pierre-Joseph Proudhon. In France, Tolstoy witnessed a public execution, which provoked in him a lifelong distrust of government and abhorrence of premeditated violence.

At the age of thirty-four, Tolstoy married Sofiya Andreyevna Behrs in 1862. She was sixteen years his junior. Sonya, as she was nicknamed, was the perfect companion to the prolific author. She ensured that the household ran smoothly so he was not bothered unnecessarily. At night, she copied his nearly inscrutable handwriting into manuscripts to be sent for publication. She took the lead in caring for their children (eventually they had thirteen).

Not long after they were married, Tolstoy began working on *War and Peace*. The massive text was his occupation for most of the 1860s. In 1873, he began to write his other great masterpiece, *Anna Karenina*, which he completed four years later. After years of struggling financially (his youthful gambling habit had depleted much of the wealth of his estate), Tolstoy found himself in possession of money, critical acclaim, and popularity with the reading public. This did not, however, make him happy; on the contrary, he sank into depression and began a spiritual search. He tried to immerse himself into Russian Orthodox Christianity, but found the Church to be corrupt. He supposed that all organized religions would be equally as prone to corruption, so he decided to work out his own beliefs, mainly focused on the teachings in Christ's Sermon on the Mount. He published his ideas in a series of religious essays. Trying to practice what he preached, Tolstoy tried to give away his possessions and wealth, much to the chagrin of his wife. In a compromise, he signed over the rights to his works to his wife. He also founded peasant schools based on his own teachings.

The Orthodox Church did not take kindly to such behavior. The Tolstoys suspected that the secret police were watching as well. Finally, in 1901, Tolstoy was excommunicated and declared anathema by the Church, and many of his former friends turned against him. His marriage had become increasingly strained in the later years of his life, and finally, in 1910, he left home one night after a quarrel with his wife, and died in a railway station on his way to a monastery.

In his later years, he wrote many pieces of literature, though none were as long as *War and Peace* or *Anna Karenina. The Death of Ivan Ilyich, The Kreutzer Sonata,* and *Resurrection* are among the most famous of his later fictional works. At one point, he had decided to give up writing fiction altogether, and only write religious and philosophical works. He could not resist writing fiction for himself, though; after his death, a novella called *Hadji Murat* was found hidden among his personal effects. The novella tells the story of a charismatic rebel commander in the Caucasus who reluctantly allies himself with Russian troops. The energetic character seems to be Tolstoy's way of trying to inspire himself to maintain his vigor even as he grew old.

Although he has always been famous for his great writings, in the late 19th and early 20th century, Tolstoy's lifestyle and writings also drew many imitators. These admirers organized into groups and communes, in what is now called the Tolstoyan movement. Tolstoy was happy to hear of the simple lives being led, and by good works such as famine relief, being done by the groups, but he emphasized that they should not focus so much on him personally. Mohandas K. Gandhi, who had corresponded with the author, founded a community in South Africa called Tolstoy Farm.

About the Summary Author

Nicole Rivett Howeson is a native of Michigan. As a teenager, she fell in love with Russian literature, and took her first university-level Russian language course while still in high school. She pursued undergraduate study at the University of Michigan and graduate study at Harvard University, both in the field of Slavic languages and literature. Nicole has traveled extensively in Europe and Russia. An academic administrator by day, she pursues writing, editing, and translation projects that allow her to share her knowledge and enthusiasm for literature, language, history, and culture. She also volunteers her time to several organizations in her community, with a particular focus on restoring the city of Detroit and improving the lives of its residents.

Notes about Names and Titles

- The Russian language is written in the Cyrillic alphabet. Over the years, the customs for transliterating Russian words into English has evolved, and to this day there is still no standard practice; therefore, every translation of *War and Peace* will spell the characters' names differently. Болконский, for example, might be rendered Bolkonski, Bolkonskii, Bolkonsky, or Bolkonskij, or Bolkonskiy, depending on the translator's preference. Some translators Anglicize the first names of the main characters instead of transliterating them; for example, Nicholas instead of Nikolai.

- Russian words, including names, have gender. Thus, a woman's surname will be different than her male relatives' because the ending will be feminine instead of masculine. That is why we have Nicholas Rostov but Natasha Rostova, and Andrew Bolkonski but Mary Bolkonskaya.

- Russians' middle names are patronymics, formed from the name of the person's father. Patronymics also have gender; for example, Andrew's patronymic is Nikolayevich, but Mary's is Nikolayevna. Anyone who meets them immediately knows that their father's name is Nicholas (Nikolay).

- Rules regarding Russian nobility titles were a bit different than those in Western Europe. "Prince" and "Princess" do not necessarily denote children of the king and queen (they have "Grand" appended to the title), but rather the old nobility descended from the ancient rulers of early Russia. Emperor Peter the Great added the titles "Count" and "Baron"—these titles could be bestowed as a person rose through the ranks of service. Titles were hereditary: all of a prince's children were princes and princesses (not just the eldest, for instance). A woman assumed her husband's title upon marriage. So, in *War and Peace*, Princess Helene Kuragina becomes Countess Bezukhova, and Countess Natasha Rostova would have been Princess Bolkonskaya, had her marriage to Andrew taken place.

Dear Amazon Customer,

Thank you for your purchase. We hope you enjoyed reading the 100-Page Summary of *War and Peace*. Our team is dedicated to your satisfaction and we want to know if your expectations were met. If for any reason you are unable to leave a favorable rating on Amazon, please email us at info@pylonpublishing.com. We want to know what we need to do to fix the problem and make a better product for all our readers. Your 100% satisfaction is our responsibility.

You can leave us feedback by following the link below or scan the QR code:

Review this book on Amazon

http://tinyurl.com/bcrlg9b

Thank you and we look forward to hearing from you.
Sincerely,

Preston
Founder, Pylon Publishing Inc.

37671990R00059

Made in the USA
San Bernardino, CA
23 August 2016